THE K.E.Y. GROUP

Keep Exploring Yourself

An Experiential Personal-Growth Group

Karen M. Finch

Association for Experiential Education

2305 Canyon Blvd., Ste. #100
Boulder, Colorado 80302

KENDALL/HUNT PUBLISHING COMPANY
4050 Westmark Drive   Dubuque, Iowa 52002

Cover design
by Maryanne Pratt

Copyright © 1996 by the Association for Experiential Education

ISBN 0-7872-2222-4

Printed in the United States of America

10 9 8 7 6 5 4 3 2 1

DEDICATED TO

Brad Finch, whose humanness always touches mine, and whose patience, honesty, and dedication to service continue to inspire my life. Thank you for your support and encouragement.

Foremost in creating the spirit of this text are the women who dared to do it differently. I have never witnessed so much courage as I have with the women at the Safehouse. Thank you, for allowing me to share my energy and passion with you, for stepping up to the line with Diane and me, and for honoring yourselves so deeply that you retrieved the voice you had once lost. May your self-love have a ripple effect upon those whose lives you touch.

ABOUT THE ASSOCIATION FOR EXPERIENTIAL EDUCATION

The Association for Experiential Education (AEE) is a not-for-profit, international, professional organization with roots in adventure education, committed to the development, practice, and evaluation of experiential learning in all settings.

AEE sponsors local, regional, and international conferences, and publishes the *Journal of Experiential Education*, the *Jobs Clearinghouse*, directories of programs and services, and a wide variety of books and periodicals to support educators, trainers, practitioners, students, and advocates.

AEE's diverse membership consists of individuals and organizations with affiliations in education, recreation, outdoor adventure programming, mental health, youth service, physical education, management development training, corrections, programming for people with disabilities, and environmental education.

To receive additional information about the Association for Experiential Education, call or write to:

AEE
2305 Canyon Blvd., Suite #100
Boulder, CO USA 80302-5651
(303) 440-8844
FAX (303) 440-9581

TABLE OF CONTENTS

DISCLAIMER

The K.E.Y. Group is intended for the use of qualified counselors facilitating an experiential personal-growth group. Training and experience in support-group theory, process, goals, models, and limitations are considered requirements before using this material. Caution should be taken in screening for participants whose greater need is for therapeutic intervention. Caution should also be exercised in using these experiential activities and adequately processing the experiences with participants. Processing questions included in each session are not all inclusive and further attempts to process what members bring up is encouraged. A co-facilitator is highly recommended to assist in leading activities and to be available should a participant need individual attention.

Although sessions are listed alphabetically, care should be taken in selecting an order that allows for a progression involving the level of trust and risk appropriate for each group. Session plans are broken down into times merely as a guide. Sufficient time and deviation from the plans will be needed to meet the needs of the group. Sixteen sessions are included for variety; the number of sessions offered to a group should be evaluated. See Section Three for more information on sequencing group sessions.

All names from group examples have been changed to protect client anonymity. All participants shown in photographs are volunteers.

ACKNOWLEDGMENTS

I have seen many women fly since the creation of this group, and I am extremely grateful to Diane Gregg for the opportunity she gave me to create and facilitate this group. I honor her wisdom, her courage, and her ability to connect with other women. She has taught me much about who I am.

And to Crossroads Safehouse for Battered Women and Their Children, for supporting our attempt to respond to the needs of these women.

I am grateful to all the authors who have granted me permission to reprint their material and offered their encouragement and words of truth. A special thank-you to Dr. Michael Gass for his time, energy, and honesty in providing feedback for me throughout this process.

I am also grateful for the hard work and dedication many have given to the field of experiential and adventure programming. This manual is possible because of the continued research, information, and creativity rapidly entering this field.

Karen M. Finch

SECTION ONE

INTRODUCTION

Photo by Tim Athey

INTRODUCTION

THE K.E.Y. GROUP

The creation of The K.E.Y. Group began in April 1994, at Crossroads Safehouse for Battered Women and Their Children, when a colleague and co-facilitator, Diane Gregg, realized the women from the community were continuing to come to our support groups around domestic violence, long after they had reached their goals. In speaking to the women, we discovered they were staying for the camaraderie with other women, the support system, and the safe place to speak their truth. Diane asked me if we could create a group to help these women fly. The answer was yes.

I began reading about specific issues and writing session plans using experiential activities. After several weeks together, the women were taking more risks in the group, sharing more deeply, supporting each other, and handling their fears with grace. By taking the focus off of domestic violence, for these particular women, they were able to fly.

I then began sharing this information with other groups, such as women's studies courses and Parents Without Partners, and in staff development trainings. The K.E.Y. Group is unique in its ability to reach men and women because of the emotional and personal issues that bind us together as human beings. During a recent closing session, a member of The K.E.Y. Group stated the impact of this group on her and recognized her power and ability to make changes in her life. In the same breath she added how sad it would be if this group were not offered to all who seek personal growth, instead of to just those who could afford it. Please facilitate this group in the spirit of these women.

WHY A PERSONAL-GROWTH GROUP?

Growth groups are made up of participants seeking the opportunity to explore and develop goals in their lives, including a greater awareness of feelings about themselves and others, changes in their lifestlyes, and improved communication skills, accomplished in an atmosphere of honest sharing and listening. Although therapy groups also try to promote growth through the process of sharing personal concerns, the role of the leader and the needs of the members are different. In a growth group, the leader functions mainly as an educator or facilitator, generating interaction among members.

By limiting the role of the facilitator, it is believed that with guidance, group members will develop the resources and ability to help themselves and one another. The K.E.Y. Group was designed as a method of allowing members to share thoughts, opinions, and experiences relevant to certain topics. Should the facilitator deem it inappropriate to focus on one member's concerns for an extended period of time, it is possible to validate the member's feelings and the issue, and to ask the member if she/he would like to speak more about that after group to allow sufficient time for all members to share.

In some respects, growth groups are more difficult to lead than support groups because there is less commonality among members. It is the facilitator's job to focus on those issues and concerns that are in some way relevant to the majority of the members.

SUGGESTIONS FOR PRESCREENING

Choosing members through an interview process based on needs, commonalities, and personal goals is essential. Prescreening questions, such as Who will the population be? How will you screen? and When should I refer people?, is the first step in facilitating a successful group. The following are sample questions important in reflecting upon future group members.

1. Why do you want to be in this group?
2. What are your expectations?
3. What concerns/topics would you like to address in the group?
4. How do you think you can contribute to the group?
5. Please write a short autobiography that describes the important events and people in your life.
6. Comment on how you feel about_____(these three topics, etc.).
7. Have you ever participated in a group of this kind before? What was your goal? What was your experience?
8. Do you have child care/transportation?

Prescreening members allows you to look for members who can work together, share, and learn from each other. A personal interview allows time to assess the appropriateness of the member, looking for dissassociative behaviors and other underlying issues that may require a more therapeutic intervention.

EVALUATION PROCESS

Forming an evaluation for members midway and/or during the final session of the group allows the members to process the experience of the group as a whole and to see how it fits into the broader picture. Providing an evaluation process also provides the facilitator with feedback on specific sessions and experiences. The following are examples of possible evaluation topics:

1. Review and summarize the group experience.
2. Assess members' growth and change.
3. How has the group applied its new skills to everyday life and implementing decisions?
4. Handling goodbyes.
5. How valuable was the experience? Scale from 1 - 10.
6. What did you like/not like about the group?
7. What did you like/not like about the way the leaders facilitated the group?
8. How could the group have been better? Elaborate on specific topics, exercises, and events that occurred during group.

QUALIFICATIONS OF A GROUP FACILITATOR

Successful use of the activities presented in The K.E.Y. Group will require an understanding of group development, experiential learning, the use of metaphors, a solution- vs. problem-focused model, and in-depth experience with processing and providing closure for a group and its members. Knowledge related to the issues of the population served and the ability to adapt The K.E.Y. Group material is essential. Please do not attempt to lead this group without the education, training, and experience needed to successfully facilitate this group and the issues that may arise.

THE K.E.Y. GROUP FORMAT

The K.E.Y. Group has evolved over the years with several different formats and time constraints. The group format presented here is what I have found most effective. Although eighteen sessions are presented, a closed group of six to eight members in a ten-week format allows for sufficient time to process experiences and explore a number of topics. Length of sessions may increase with the number of participants to allow for sufficient time to reflect.

Topics are listed in alphabetical order, but I do not recommend leading them in that order. Section Three in this manual contains several recommendations for sequencing these activities with various types of groups. Members should be screened for appropriateness, making referrals for those whose immediate need is therapeutic intervention. Based on the group and the background of members, sessions should be arranged according to building skill level and trust in the group. Evaluation of each group by a qualified counselor is essential.

For more information on sequencing activities and building trust in a group, refer to: *Islands of Healing*, Schoel, Prouty, & Radcliffe (1988), pages 65-85.

THE FOLLOWING IS THE FORMAT FOR EACH SESSION IN THE K.E.Y. GROUP:

RELAXATION EXERCISES

Each session begins with a relaxation exercise to bring members to the present moment and to help ground and focus them. Teaching them techniques of breathing, and of stilling their minds and their chatterboxes (or internal voices), is important to decrease their physical pain resultant from holding tension, and to increase their ability to stay conscious in the moment.

CIRCLE OF PERSONAL POWER

"Power" refers to the qualities inside of us that enable us to take care of ourselves, without hurting or taking responsibity for others. It is within our "power" to create our lives on a daily basis. For the *Circle of Personal Power*, each week a different member brings to group an object (thought, picture, poem) they deem important and personally meaningful, and they share the power it holds. The object is then laid in the middle of the circle for members to begin sharing their immediate thoughts or feelings at that time. The goal of the Circle is to listen without responding. Members are asked to simply hear what the others are saying without the distraction of formulating their next thought, or trying to comfort or solve another's emotions. As each member receives the object, she/he speaks from the heart, sharing what they are experiencing (thinking, feeling, seeing) at that moment.   Members found this type of sharing particularly powerful because they felt challenged not to respond, to listen without taking away another's pain. They also felt freer to speak. This became such a powerful and calming experience for the group, that eventually we no longer used the relaxation exercises. During a session on "Empowerment," the group identified forty-two of their powers. Each session in The K.E.Y. Group is a session on these powers. Our goal in the group is to raise awareness of our powers, and hence what we are responsible for and have control over, and to experience them and respond to them throughout the group and beyond.

ADDRESSING THE TOPIC/EXPERIENTIAL ACTIVITY

An activity serves as the main focus for addressing how each specific topic relates to our lives. Facilitation guides are included for each activity. Though only one way to facilitate these exercises is presented, many books have been written on facilitating experiential activities and the role of the facilitators. Successful use of these activities will require an understanding of the basis of group development, experiential education, use of metaphors, a solution- vs.

problem-focused model, and processing or debriefing an experience. Please adhere to the safety precautions outlined.

PROCESSING THE EXPERIENCE

Processing questions are included with each session, though are not intended to be inclusive. I have written about the issues the groups have brought up, committed to helping them understand the solution is inside of them. The K.E.Y. Group strongly emphasizes tools in each session, concrete tools members can learn and use—when they remain conscious to the present moment. Processing these experiences is of upmost importance in experiential learning as processing can be the key to transferring what was experienced in group to its relevance in one's daily life. See additional information on processing in ADDRESSING THE TOPIC in Section Two of this manual.

CLOSURE/HANDOUTS

Each session ends with a closure activity. Journaling has been very effective in allowing the members to express themselves and see their own growth throughout the group. Closure allows for goals to be set around each issue, and for members to ask for support from others. Handouts included are helpful in allowing members to reflect upon past topics and serve as affirmations and tools in their lives.

SECTION TWO

ADDRESSING THE TOPIC/EXPERIENTIAL ACTIVITIES

Photo by Tim Athey

ADDRESSING THE TOPIC/EXPERIENTIAL ACTIVITIES

The K.E.Y. Group was created with experiential learning and the use of metaphors in mind. A clear understanding of group development, experiential learning, how to process experience, and the use of metaphors to address different learning modalities (auditory, visual, and kinesthetic), as well as a working knowledge of a solution- vs. problem-focused model and experience in the counseling field are highly recommended as prerequisites for leading this group. The following is a brief synopsis of the theories behind The K.E.Y. Group.

GROUP DEVELOPMENT MODEL

There are forces present in any group situation. Members want to feel accepted by other group members, feel they belong, feel safe, and know what is expected. When these forces are lacking in a group, members tend to be negative, withdrawn, or apathetic. It is also the tendency of all groups to go through some predictable stages of growth and regression. Tuckerman (1965) summarized the results of over fifty studies into the following four-stage model of group development:

Stage I: Form
It is during the first few sessions of a group that members discover what behaviors are acceptable to the group. Members are looking for guidance in a new environment; thus, members may be hesitant to participate, they may experience fear, suspicion, or anxiety about the new situation, and there will be attempts to identify how the group will accomplish tasks.

Stage II: Storm
Conflict characterizes this stage as members begin to express their individuality and resist group formation. Disunity, defensiveness, and polarization of group members is common as members begin to recognize the extent of the demands, responding emotionally to the perceived requirements for self-change and self-denial.

Stage III: Norm
It is during this stage that members begin accepting the group, group norms, their roles, and individuality. Emotional conflict is reduced by resolving conflicts within relationships. Confusion over the group's purpose and priorities sets in as the group starts to realign. There may be an increased level of intimacy among members, characterized by confiding in each other and sharing

personal problems. A sense of team cohesiveness emerges with a common spirit and goal. Boundaries begin to form.

Stage IV: Perform

Entering this stage with group norms established, the group becomes capable of identifying and solving problems, as well as making decisions. Increased awareness and insight may occur as well as constructive self-change. Stage IV is not always reached by all groups.

Just as individuals go through predictable stages of growth depending on age, experience, maturity, etc., the ability of the group to travel through these stages depends on factors such as individual and group maturity, leadership in the group, and the external climate. Groups can become fixated in a stage, like some people, and never fully function. Sharing concerns and expectations about the group early on, and minimizing the tension, fear, and anxiety common in the first stages, may reduce the time needed for groups to procede through these phases. Understanding the progression of trust activities in a group and following a slow progression of emotional risk will contribute to the success, allowing members to move on to performing.

EXPERIENTIAL LEARNING

Experiential learning is founded on many principles, including behavior change, or learning, occurring when people are placed outside of their normal range of comfort. Challenged to regain this comfort state, growth and learning are achieved through personal motivation, involvement, and responsibility (Gass, 1993). Other principles inherent in experiential learning include the active versus the passive role of the participants, the real and meaningful activities employed that hold present as well as future relevance to the participant, and the crucial role of reflection in experiential learning. Also referred to as processing or debriefing, reflection allows a participant to internalize and generalize an experience, and to seek ways it might be useful in the future (Priest, 1989).

Simple participation in an experience, however, does not make it experiential.   Chapman, McPhee, and Proudman (1992) suggested ten principles, in varying degrees, which must be present sometime during the experiential learning.

    1. **Mixture of Content and Process**
        The integration of experience and theory.

    2. **Absence of Excessive Teacher Judgment**
        Teachers recognize the effects of their conditioning in order to allow
        students to have their own experiences minus the teacher's judgment.

3. **Engaged in Purposeful Endeavors**

 There needs to be meaning for the student in the learning and it needs to be personally relevant.

4. **Encouraging the Big Picture Perspective**

 Experiential methodology provides opportunities for the student to see and feel their relationships with the broader world.

5. **Teaching with Multiple Learning Styles**

 Emphasizes that for a person to learn experientially, a teaching routine must include a cycle of all four learning styles (Kolb, 1976): concrete, abstract, conceptualization, and active experimentation.

6. **Role of Reflection**

 The dissonance created in mixing experience with associated content and guided reflection allows learners the opportunities to bring the theory to life and gain valuable insights about themselves and their interactions with the world at large.

7. **Creating an Emotional Investment**

 Creating an environment where people are fully valued and appreciated; learners' motivations to continue are no longer based on what they have to do, they become immersed in their own learning experience.

8. **Re-examination of Values**

 When participants feel valued and appreciated, there is greater likelihood that they will re-examine and explore their own values.

9. **Presence of Meaningful Relationships**

 Learning is fully embraced when it is experienced as a series of relationships—learner to self, learner to teacher, and learner to learning environment.

10. **Learning Outside of One's Perceived Comfort Zone**

 Learner often needs to be challenged in order to be stretched by a new experience. Comfort zone refers to the physical environment as well as the social environment (i.e., being accountable for one's actions and owning the consequences).

 (p. 21)

Experiential learning balances concrete experiences with reflection and observation, so neither dominates the experience. Self-discovery is encouraged through the facilitator's accepting and non-judgmental attitude, through participants' involvement with ideas, people, problem solving, and risk taking when the experience becomes challenging and stressful. Chapman, McPhee, and Proudman (1992) also suggest that through this process of self-discovery, participants become personally and emotionally involved in the activities, exploring and challenging their current abilities and values.

Experiential learning is a cycle beginning with direct experiences, followed by sharing and expressing aspects of what happened in an experience, generalizing principles and what may be applicable to other situations, and applying what was learned to new situations. Kolb (1984) suggested that the most meaningful learning will go through this cycle.

For more information on experiential learning, see:
Kolb (1984), Knapp (1992), Chapman, McPhee, & Proudman (1992), and Gass (1985).

USE OF METAPHOR

Since the beginning of time, stories and metaphors have been used to pass on important traditions and learning about life, and have been found in most cultures (Gordon, 1978). The metaphor is a form of symbolic language used for centuries as a method of teaching in various fields. Stories have motivated people, causing them to recall, reflect on, and explore new ideas. Stories have served as models for behaviors, thoughts, and feelings. As the focus of personal growth is on helping people to become motivated for action, embracing new ideas and reflecting on the world from different perspectives, the use of stories and metaphors seems logical.

Atwood and Levine (1990) defined metaphor as a process whereby meaning is transferred from one situation to another that is in some way similar. The power of a metaphor comes from the ability to approach a problem indirectly: "Because metaphors do not state things 'as they are,' they tend to bypass conscious reflexive objections to ideas and interventions " (Bowman, 1992, p. 440). Zeig and Gilligan (1990) state that the metaphor frees the client, allowing her/him to assign meaning and to choose the most useful interpretation. The challenge in using metaphors lies in asking members to relate to an issue through a metaphor with their right brain, and interpreting it with their left. The fundamental idea behind the use of metaphors is to allow clients to recognize that they have options.

Emotions elicited during an activity, such as confusion, anxiety, stress, and discomfort, can be helpful tools of change since participants strive to bring these emotions back into their normal range of comfort (Gass, 1993). Experiential activities use metaphors such as blindfolding, loss of voice, or limited use of one's arms or legs to elicit these emotions and provide opportunity for reflecting upon similar experiences in life.

For more information on designing metaphors to meet the needs of clients, see:
Gass (1991, 1993), Priest & Gass (1993, 1994), Gass & Gillis (1995), and Bacon (1987, 1983.)

PREFERRED SENSORY REPRESENTATION SYSTEMS

To be effective, the metaphor must be matched with the specific needs of the individual. Bandler and Grinder (1975) proposed that individuals preferred certain sensory representation systems in characterizing their experiences, and that problems were unique to a specific system. They suggested people have preferred modes for taking in, storing, and recalling information based on the visual, auditory, and kinesthetic senses. A person's preferred mode can be identified by the sensory words in their actual speech. For example, the statements, "that **sounds** right," "I can **see** what you are saying," and "that **rubs** me the wrong way," represent the respective modalities. Metaphors, to be most effective, must be designed to best fit the primary modality of the client (Atwood & Levine, 1990).

AUDITORY

Storytelling and simple phrases or words are helpful in matching metaphors to people who frequently use auditory sounds to perceive their world. Gordon (1978) noted that some characters in great adventure stories, like *Alice in Wonderland* or *Odysseus*, are really metaphors for all of us in the way they use their personal resources when they are confronted with problems. Clients identify with the struggle and successful resolution of the character's problems. Other examples also try to frame the metaphor to fit the client's internal world. This metaphor from Hendrix (1992) is useful in explaining the principle of learned helplessness.

> This elephant metaphor is lead into by asking if the client knows how elephants are trained. Usually the answer is negative. The counselor points out that it is impossible for a 200-pound human to restrain an 8,000-pound elephant, but in actuality, humans do control elephants. Elephants are taught to accept the trainer's control through learned helplessness. The elephant's back leg is chained to a large tree. The elephant pulls repeatedly at the chain but cannot get loose. Eventually, the animal gives up. After that occurs, the elephant can be restrained anywhere by simply chaining its leg and attaching the chain to a stake. The elephant could easily pull the stake out of the ground and escape, but it feels the chain and does not try. (p. 236)

VISUAL

Metaphoric objects have been found useful in working with clients whose visual representation system is more dominant when perceiving the world around them (Angus & Rennie, 1988.) This metaphor, by Jooste and Cleaver (1992), was used with a client who appeared to be unsure of herself and felt incapable of revealing her own thoughts and emotions. She had difficulty giving meaning to her existence.

> The counselor presented the client with a tangled ball of wool made up of many strands of different colors and in a state of disorder. The softness of the wool represented the vulnerability of the client. The state of disorder meant that the wool could not, at the present time, be utilized but that it had the potential of becoming useful to the client. (p. 141)

Other ways of using visual metaphors are found in guided imagery: changing the colors, size, background, sequence, and number and nature of the objects presented (Bandler, 1985).

KINESTHETIC

Metaphors that appeal to people who use the kinesthetic sense —or sense of touch—to experience and perceive their world, make use of activities where the client is physically and emotionally involved. The activity used in the session entitled "Perceptions of Self" illustrates the kinesthetic concept in a concrete way. It asks members to use a piece of clay or playdough to mold two figures, one of which should represent how they perceive themselves, the other how they believe others perceive them. This activity requires the right brain to participate and form such a perception without words. The client is able to express her/himself through touch and creativity. Physically engaged in the activity, people who perceive their world from a kinesthetic view prefer hands-on and touch experiences.

The above-mentioned activities and initiatives are of a cooperative nature and promote trust, problem solving, and cohesion among group members. Gillis and Bonney (1986) state that the metaphor may be the most powerful function of adventure activities because real-life problems can be focused on and strategically reframed. Whether the objective is to encourage or discourage a particular behavior, the metaphor used must reflect this content. The key to the successful use of metaphors is the appropriate reframing of the behavior (Strong, 1989). Several studies have indicated the advantage of incorporating metaphors into client interventions. Erickson (1980) and Haley (1973) found that using metaphors versus confrontation or suggestions, reduced client defenses toward functional change. In accordance with the belief that the right hemisphere is used to process metaphorical communication, imagery, and emotions (Lucia, 1973), it has been theorized that because symptoms are expressions of language from the right hemisphere, the use of metaphoric language must be used in order to communicate directly to the right hemisphere in its own language.

With the understanding that people perceive the world in different ways, whether through sound, vision, or feeling, facilitators can choose the most relevant form of expression and then lead clients to stay with that sense and experience the expression more fully (Araoz, 1985).

PROCESSING THE EXPERIENCE

Processing, also referred to as debriefing or reflecting, involves a guided reflection of behaviors, issues, feelings, emotions, and attitudes around the experience (Quinsland & Van Ginkel, 1984). Processing, one of the most valuable skills of a facilitator, may be where the fundamental learning resulting from the experience occurs. The exercise or activity stimulates members' reactions, but it is the facilitator's guiding statements that will help cause members to personalize the experience.

Processing can be verbal or non-verbal (such as through journaling or drawing) and may go through several levels:

1) THE ACTIVITY ITSELF

What was the easiest/most difficult, interesting, fun, scariest part of the activity for you? What did you see? What part of the reading stood out to you? Describe your drawing to us.

2) HOW THE ACTIVITY AFFECTED THE GROUP

What did you learn about someone in the group that you did not know already? What would you like to say to someone as a result of doing this activity? What question would you like to ask the group?

3) FEELINGS, THOUGHTS, OR INSIGHTS GENERATED BY THE ACTIVITY

What did you learn about yourself? What are you more aware of because of this activity or experience? What feelings were generated by the activity?

4) HOW THE EXERCISE RELATES TO LIFE OUTSIDE THE GROUP

How will you use what you learned tomorrow? How does your reaction to this activity relate to another part of your life right now? What are some things you would like to do now after experiencing and discussing these issues?

For each group, the types of processing questions utilized will vary depending upon the purpose of the group, needs of the members, the communication and cognitive processing skills of the members, and the abilities of the leader. Processing will not necessarily develop in the order above, and not all levels may be explored with every group and every exercise. The facilitator must monitor the direction of processing to determine if it fits the needs and purposes of the group.

Processing is an art, and requires practice and knowledge of the variety of ways to reflect upon an experience. For more information on processing an experience and alternative ways to process, see: Gass (1993), Schoel, Prouty, & Radcliffe (1988), Knapp (1989, 1992), Nadler & Luckner (1992), and Priest & Gass (1993, 1994).

SOLUTION- VS. PROBLEM-FOCUSED MODEL

When operating from a solution-focused model, reflection focuses on what participants are doing well and what behaviors are supporting that success. Choosing to focus on the exception to the problem (the solution), versus what behaviors cause and maintain the problem, validates the creative, inner resources of a participant.

  Examples of solution-focused processing include:
> From whom are you unable to ask for what you need?
> Are there times when you <u>are</u> able to ask for what you need from that person? When?
> Are there people from whom you can ask for what you need?
> What difference frees you to ask?

Frontloading an activity (Priest & Gass, 1994) asks participants to consider possible growth areas that may occur in the activity.

  Examples of solution-focused frontloading include:
> Can you, as a group, identify behaviors that may lead you to success in this activity?
> What can you do to make communication clear amongst yourselves?

Scaling is a processing technique (Berg, 1994) where the facilitator asks the participants to rate their abilities on a scale. In a solution-focused approach, we are looking for what the participant did well in order to obtain that number (even if it's a 3, the client is doing something to keep it from being a 1). A solution-focused approach highlights what members are already doing well and encourages the solution behavior.

Examples of solution-focused scaling include:

> On a scale from 0 to 10, how well did you communicate your needs in that situation (activity, etc.)?

For more information on a solution- vs. problem-focused model, see: Gass & Gillis (1995) and de Shazer (1985, 1988).

The importance of understanding the stages a group goes through, as well as the tenets of experiential learning, the use of metaphor, and the need to practice reflection with a solution-focused approach, is key to facilitating a successful group. Each of these topics is only minimally addressed, as there are books available on each topic. The integration of these concepts is what The K.E.Y. Group was founded on and is presented through. Processing and becoming comfortable changing session plans mid-flight is the sign of an experienced facilitator and is needed in a group of this type. Please know your limitations and do not bring the group where you cannot go. Those who are seasoned in group facilitation skills will find The K.E.Y. Group an enjoyable and challenging group to facilitate as the material is personal and emotional for all of us.

SECTION THREE

SAMPLE PROGRESSIONS FOR GROUPS

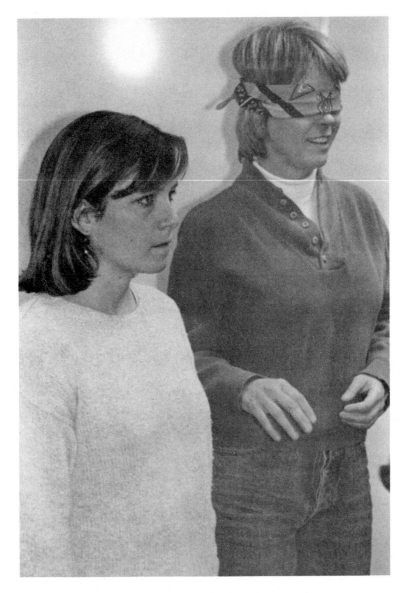

Photo by Tim Athey

SAMPLE PROGRESSIONS FOR GROUPS

The progression you choose with groups will depend upon many factors:
> population
> number of participants
> cognitive and communication level of participants
> maturity level of participants
> number of sessions lead
> purpose of group

From my experience, it has been most effective (interest, attendance, and participation maintained) to lead eight to ten sessions, with 6-8 participants. With this number, we have been able to allow ample sharing and processing time, without remaining on a superficial level due to time constraints. It is crucial to provide a progression of sessions leading up to trust and cohesion in a group. Beginning with the session on trust is not recommended as the level of trust in the group has not been earned. Verbal activities requiring speaking, followed by touching and sharing more personal issues, is recommended to develop trust within the group.

The following are the sixteen sessions (disregarding the opening and closing sessions) in the order of risk (emotional and physical). Choosing from the beginning of the list where the activities are less threatening in nature will encourage the ability of your group members to share and participate at their own pace. After this list are sample sessions for a variety of groups.

LOW-RISK FACTORS: Asking For What We Need
> **Boundaries**
> **Finding a Balance**
> **Self-Love**

These activities are low in risk because they involve activities such as guided imagery and sharing, and sharing where members can choose how much they share about themselves. They are also sessions that do not involve touching or physically depending upon another person.

MEDIUM-RISK FACTORS:　　　Depression
　　　　　　　　　　　　　　　Empowerment
　　　　　　　　　　　　　　　Expressing Feelings
　　　　　　　　　　　　　　　Fear
　　　　　　　　　　　　　　　Self-Love

These particular sessions are considered medium risk because of the nature of the topic as well as the emotions that may be stirred up. I have led sessions on empowerment where members have become angry and have felt many other conflicting and powerful emotions after realizing what's been happening in their lives. Waking people up can prove to be eventful. Be prepared. These activities do not involve physically touching each other, but the level of sharing becomes greater and more risky.

HIGH-RISK FACTORS:　　　On Being A Woman
　　　　　　　　　　　　　Defending Ourselves
　　　　　　　　　　　　　Perceptions of Self
　　　　　　　　　　　　　Relationships
　　　　　　　　　　　　　Trust

These sessions have continually elicited emotions and issues in group members over the years. Activities requiring physical touch and personal sharing are presented, as well as added feedback between group members. Many participants find it difficult to hear other people's views of them even after compassion and trust have been experienced.

Groups with common backgrounds/experiences:

Opening Session # 1
Boundaries
Asking For What You Need
Empowerment
Fear
Depression As An Opportunity for Growth
Relationships
Perceptions of Self
Trust
Closing Session #1

Groups with diverse backgrounds, but similar goals of personal growth:

Opening Session #2
Boundaries
Finding a Balance
Defending Ourselves
Empowerment
Fear
On Being A Woman
Trust
Perceptions of Self
Closing Session #2

As a common practice, I hand out the list of 14 topics to participants at the end of the first session and ask them to pick the top five topics they would like to explore in group. I pull the rest of the sessions from their choices, coupled with my own sense of what would work well with that particular group. It is done at the end of the first session so members have a chance to get to know the facilitators and other members, while getting a feel for what kind of energy they want to put into the group. Most importantly, asking for their imput fosters a sense of ownership in the group.

It is difficult to write a prescription for each type of group due to the diversity of personalities, skills, and maturity among members. The ability to be spontaneous and flexible enough to deviate from the session plans will be a facilitator's greatest strength. Evaluating sessions, checking in with members, and having a co-facilitator to share the experience with is the best prescription for success I can give you.

SECTION FOUR

THE K.E.Y. GROUP SESSION PLANS

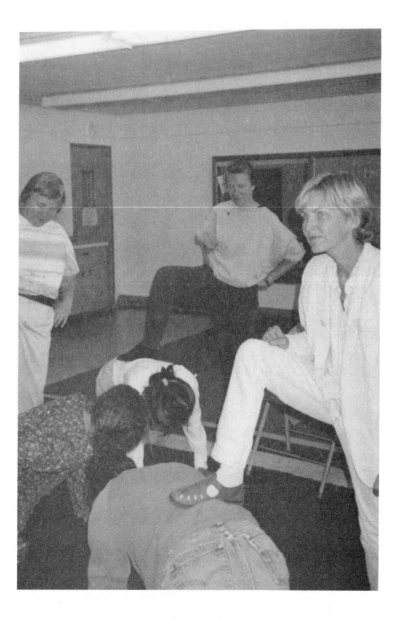

Photo by Tim Athey

OPENING SESSION #1

Purpose of Session:
1. Introduction of members and facilitators
2. Clarification of purpose, goals, and expectations
3. Discussion of group norms
4. Begin to establish trust, cohesion, and commitment through sharing

<u>Time</u>	<u>Activity</u>	<u>Purpose</u>
5 minutes	Introduction of facilitators and The K.E.Y. Group. Share the principles The K.E.Y. Group was founded on and emphasize the focus on **SELF** and the **KEY** to growth. Clarify your role as a facilitator.	Introduce the purpose and history of the K.E.Y. Group.
10 minutes	Activity: Drawing Our Names	Allows the expression of "who we are." Asks members to go beyond the familiar.
20 minutes	Sharing our names, who we are, and two things you'd like to be able to add to your drawing by the time the group ends.	Begin sharing who we are and how we see ourselves.
15 minutes	Establish the group norms and what members need from each other in order to feel safe in the group. Read "Participant Rights" by Jackie Gerstein and discuss what members and facilitators need from the group.	Begin to increase commitment and ownership of the group.

20 minutes	Activity: Journal Making and writing in journals. Why are you in this group? What do you hope to gain from it? What are you willing to do?	Begin to establish commitment in the group by making and decorating a personal journal to be used throughout the group to sort through thoughts, feelings, and ideas.
15 minutes	Process: In a round, share why members are in the group and what some of their goals may be.	Through sharing, members begin to link common experiences, emotions, and goals. Formulates topics for future sessions.
5 minutes	Closure. How are you feeling about the group so far?	Allow members to express comfort level, conflicts, and gains.

MATERIALS NEEDED:

Paper
Drawing utensils
Board or Pad (to list group norms)
Marker
Pens

For Journals: Covering (parchment paper, etc.)
Paper (for inside)
Large Needles
Scissors
Plastic Straw or Ribbon (to thread with)

DIRECTIONS FOR JOURNALS:

Cut covering slightly larger than paper. Fold covering and paper in half. Punch three holes with needle in center of fold. Thread needle from outside to inside, up through the middle, down opposite side, and back through the middle. Tie ends off on outside of journal. This set-up allows for adding additional paper if needed.

PARTICIPANT BILL OF RIGHTS

* I have the right to confidentiality and privacy by the facilitators and other group members.

* I have the right to choose to participate or not participate in any of the activities or discussions.

* I have the right to be treated with respect by the other group members.

* I have the right to ask for and receive physical and emotional support from the other group members.

* I have the right to express my feelings, thoughts and opinions.

* I have the right to be listened to and taken seriously.

* I have the right to make mistakes.

* I have the right to celebrate personal and group successes.

* I have the right to say, "I don't understand."

* I have the right to say, "No!"

* I have the right to remain silent or "pass" during group discussions.

* I have the right to decide how and who will enter into my body area.

* I have the right NOT to have the values of others for ced on me.

* I have the right NOT to be exposed by excess pressure from the other group members.

OPENING SESSION #2

Purpose of Session:
1. Introduction of members and facilitators
2. Clarification of purpose, goals, and expectations
3. Discussion of group norms and participant rights
4. Begin to establish trust, cohesion, and commitment through sharing

Time	Activity	Purpose
5 minutes	Introduction of facilitators and The K.E.Y. Group. Introduce the principles The K.E.Y. Group was founded on and emphasize the focus on **SELF** and the **KEY** to growth.	Introduce the facilitators, history, and purpose of the group.
20 minutes	Activity: Name Game. Ask each member to state their name, how they got it, who they were named after, any nicknames, and if they ever desired a different name.	Begin to share and learn about each other in a fun, non-threatening way.
15 minutes	Clarify the roles of facilitators and discuss interests and expectations of the members. What do they need from the group in order to feel safe? Read "Participant Rights" together and discuss how much protection is needed by members in the group. What topics do they hope to explore?	Clarify needs and expectations of members and establish norms to which members agree to adhere.
15 minutes	Activity : Journal Making	Increase commitment to group by creating a personal journal to record thoughts, feelings, and ideas throughout the group.

10 minutes	Activity: Writing in Journals. Ask members to identify what they feel have been their strengths in life; what about them has helped through difficult times in their lives? Ask also what members hope to achieve through The K.E.Y. Group and what they are willing to do to reach those goals.	Begin to ask members to look closer at themselves, through journaling. Writing also serves to assist members in formulating thoughts before sharing with the group.
20 minutes	Sharing our journals. Sharing our strengths and how we can use those strengths in group, as well as our goals for being here.	Through sharing, members begin to link common experiences, emotions, and goals. Begin to share on a deeper level.
5 minutes	Closure. How are you feeling about the group so far? Any questions, concerns, or comments? (Option to pass out journals pre-made to allow members to reflect on today and future groups.)	Allow members to express their comfort level and any concerns they may have.

MATERIALS NEEDED:

Paper (for inside journal)
Parchment Paper (for covering)
Scissors
Large Needles
Plastic Straw or Ribbon (to thread with)

DIRECTIONS FOR JOURNALS:

Cut covering slightly larger than paper. Fold covering and paper in half. Punch three holes with needle in center of fold. Thread needle from outside to inside, up through the middle, down opposite side, and back through the middle. Tie ends off on outside of journal. This set-up allows for adding additional paper if needed.

PARTICIPANT BILL OF RIGHTS

* I have the right to confidentiality and privacy by the facilitators and other group members.

* I have the right to choose to participate or not participate in any of the activities or discussions.

* I have the right to be treated with respect by the other group members.

* I have the right to ask for and receive physical and emotional support fro m the other group members.

* I have the right to express my feelings, thoughts and opinions.

* I have the right to be listened to and taken seriously.

* I have the right to make mistakes.

* I have the right to celebrate personal and group successes.

* I have the right to say, "I don't understand."

* I have the right to say, "No!"

* I have the right to remain silent or "pass" during group discussions.

* I have the right to decide how and who will enter into my body area.

* I have the right NOT to have the values of others forced on me.

* I have the right NOT to be exposed by excess pressure from the other group members.

ASKING FOR WHAT YOU NEED

Purpose of Session:
1. Gain a different perspective on needs members are experiencing
2. Guided imagery
3. Exploring what's enabled us to ask for what we need
4. Create a visual metaphor for members to reflect upon

Time	Activity	Purpose
5 minutes	Centering Activity: Group Massage Ask members to form a circle standing, or sitting, and to massage the person's shoulders in front of them. Use soft music and ask for silence to begin to ground members and bring about their awareness to the here and now.	Focus members and involve members in creating a relaxed and supportive atmosphere.
15 minutes	Circle of Personal Power	Allow members to share immediate thoughts and feelings.
15 minutes	What happens in your family/relationship when you ask for what you need? When do you ask for what you need? What is it that keeps you from asking for what you need?	Introduce topic of asking for what we need. Ask members to reflect on times they have asked, and how often they ask.

10 minutes	Activity: Animal Fantasy Guided Imagery (Facilitation guide on following page)	Create a visual metaphor—an animal that represents a **need**—so that members may step back and gain awareness of what they need to ask for.
15 minutes	Process: Dyads or triads. Share your animal. What is the essence of the animal you can identify with? What did you need from each other? What will it take for that exchange of needs to transpire? Where did you feel it the strongest in your body?	Share with others their experience and insight. Offer support and validation for their needs.
20 minutes	Activity: List on the Board: What allows us to ask for what we need? What conditions, qualities, skills, etc., enable us to ask for what we need?	Establishes an awareness of what needs to happen for members to express themselves. Provides a positive frame of reference.
10 minutes	Closure: What two strengths do you and the animal you chose share? How can you use those strengths when asking for what you need? Encourage members to journal their experience.	End with positive affirmations of one's strengths and how to apply this session to the future.

MATERIALS NEEDED:
Journals
Pens
Board or Pad
Chalk or Markers

Animal Fantasy Guided Imagery

Position yourself comfortably. Close your eyes if you are comfortable doing that, and begin to relax your body. Take a deep breath in and hold it. Let it out slowly. Take another deep breath. Feel your eyes and jaw relax. Feel, as you breathe, your shoulders loosen and your hands go limp. Allow your body to relax. Feel the chair surround your body, and become aware of your body.

PAUSE

Dream you are in a quiet, safe place. Notice your surroundings.

PAUSE

Begin to think of a current situation or one appearing in the near future, where you will need to ask for what you need. Now picture an animal. It is usually the first animal that pops into your mind, and this animal will represent this situation. Think about where the animal is: in the wilderness, in the air, underwater? Is it alone or with other animals? With people? What are its characteristics? What is the nature of the animal?

PAUSE

Breathe in and let it out slowly. The animal begins to approach you. Continue to breathe. The animal will ask you what you need from it. If you need something from it, then tell it what you need. If you need nothing, then convey that as well.

PAUSE

Now ask the animal what it needs from you. If it needs something, then let it tell you what it needs. If the animal needs nothing, then let it convey that, too.

PAUSE

Summarize in your mind the animal you have chosen, what the animal needs from you, and what you need from it.

PAUSE

Now become aware of your body at this moment. Where in your body is the feeling the strongest? Where do you feel it when you have asked for what you need? Is it in your head, your eyes, or your ears? Do you feel it in your chest or your stomach? Your legs or your feet? Where do you feel it the most?

Take a deep breath and allow the animal to leave. Open your eyes when you are ready.

ASKING FOR WHAT WE NEED

Decide what it is you want and need, then go to the person you need it from and ask for it.

Sometimes, it takes hard work and much energy to get what we want and need. We have to go through the pains of identifying what we want, then struggle to believe that we deserve it. Then, we may have to experience the disappointment of asking someone, having the person refuse us, and figuring out what to do next.

Sometimes in life, getting what we want and need is not so difficult. Sometimes, all we need to do is ask.

We can go to another person, or our Higher Power, and ask for what we need.

But because of how difficult it can be, at times, to get what we want and need, we may get trapped in the mind-set of believing it will always be that difficult. Sometimes, not wanting to go through the hassle, dreading the struggle, or out of fear, we may make getting what we want and need much more difficult than it needs to be.

We may get angry before we ask, deciding that we'll never get what we want, or anticipating the "fight" we'll have to endure. By the time we talk to someone about what we want, we may be so angry that we're demanding, not asking; thus our anger triggers a power play that didn't exist except in our mind.

Or we may get so worked up that we don't ask—or we waste far more energy than necessary fighting with ourselves, only to find out the other person, or our Higher Power, is happy to give us what we want.

Sometimes, we have to fight and work and wait for what we want and need. Sometimes, we can get it just by asking or stating that this is what we want. Ask. If the answer is no, or not what we want, *then* we can decide what to do next.

Today, I will not set up a difficult situation that doesn't exist with other people, or my Higher Power, about getting what I want and need. If there is something I need from someone, I will ask first, before I struggle.

ON BEING A WOMAN

Purpose of Session:
1. Explore what it means to be a woman
2. Explore feelings around body image and touch
3. Explore ways to celebrate being a woman

Time	Activity	Purpose
5 minutes	Centering Activity: A Guided Imagery	Assist members in becoming focused and present centered.
15 minutes	Circle of Personal Power	Allow members time to share immediate thoughts and feelings
20 minutes	Activity: Sculpture Ask members to express feelings as they arise during the activity to help members work through the feelings. (Facilitation guide on following page)	Experiential activity used to explore being touched, our personal space, and our body image.
20 minutes	Process: Which role—model, sculptor, or clay—was the most comfortable for you? Most uncomfortable, and why? What is your comfort level with touch in other areas of your life, with strangers, family, friends? At what point in your life did that comfort level change?	Explore the comfort levels members have around touch, and how that may relate to body image. Explore what, if anything, changed their level of comfort in their lives.

25 minutes	Share "The Body in the Mirror." Share *Circle of Stones*. Share the significance of women and the moon, and the cycle we share. Explore ways to celebrate being a woman.	Bring awareness of celebrating the body we have and ways to celebrate being a woman.
5 minutes	Closing: Journal what members have experienced and become aware of in this session on being a woman.	Allow members time to journal their experience, feelings, thoughts, and goals.

MATERIALS NEEDED:

Journals

Pens

Rope (or other means to mark a circle)

DIRECTIONS FOR SCULPTURE:

This activity involves being touched and being blindfolded. The degree of emotional risk is high and judgment should be used when applying it to groups with issues around being touched. Blindfolds are optional. Ask members to close their eyes. Closing one's eyes versus the leader blindfolding them, gives members more control and power.

Ask members to get into groups of three. This activity requires members to play three roles: **The Model** will choose a position to stand or sit that she/he can comfortably maintain. **The Sculptor,** eyes closed or blindfolded, will be given as much time as needed to discover, through touch, what position the model is in and then will sculpt **The Clay** to that position. Once leaving, the Sculptor cannot return to the Model for the remainder of the activity. As time allows, ask members to switch roles.

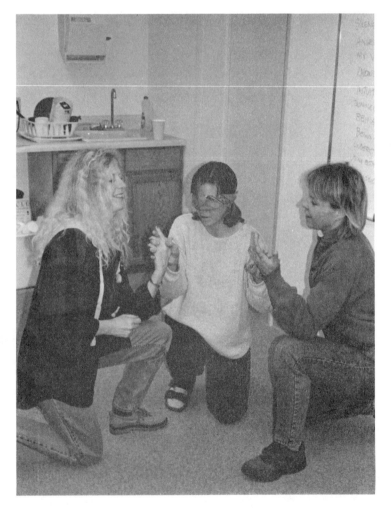

Photo by Tim Athey

CENTERING
-a guided imagery-

This exercise will assist you in two primary ways. First, you will experience yourself slowing down. This makes it easier to focus your attention. Second, you will experience your "center" which is defined here as your core of wisdom, love, and compassion, your inherent goodness.

Get as comfortable as you can, close your eyes and take several deep breaths. Feel the air as it enters your body, fills your body, and leaves your body.

PAUSE

Now shift your awareness to your body... can you feel the outline of your body as it rests against whatever you are resting on? If you feel discomfort in some part of your body, and if you need to move to release it, do so...

Now shift your awareness to your feelings... What are you feeling right now?... calm, anxiety, anger, joy?... Where are you feeling this feeling?... What would be the opposite of this feeling? Can you be aware of yourself in order to recognize and know it?... Where in your body do you feel this opposite feeling?

PAUSE

And now, shift your awareness to your mind... How are you able to see your mind?... Who is it that is able to see your mind? Just observe the activity that is going on in your mind right now.

PAUSE

Now focus on the word **center** and on the concept **center**... and now on the experience of **center**... Has your attention shifted to that place or feeling that is your center?... If not, focus there now and just experience your center as fully as possible... Can you become aware of the energy, the vitality, the life that is your center?... See if you can feel that...

PAUSE

And now, let that energy begin to grow, to expand and move through your body. Feel it in your back, in your shoulders, your abdomen, your chest, upper arms, forearms and hands... Can you feel this energy in your legs, your feet... how about in your toes?... Can you feel it in your neck, your scalp, your face?... See if you can feel this energy throughout your entire body all at once.

PAUSE

Are you shifting your attention from place to place in your body to experience this feeling?... or have you moved back from yourself in order to feel it everywhere at once?... Look to see how you are experiencing this feeling.

PAUSE

Continue to focus on this life force, this vitality throughout your body... where do you feel it most strongly?... Do you know how you are able to experience this feeling?... see if you can increase the feeling, intensify the sensation....

Stay with this experience for as long as you like, and when you are ready, bring your attention back into the room, and slowly open your eyes.

From *The Depression Book. Depression as an Opportunity for Growth.* Pages 76-79.
Copyright 1991 by A Center for Zen Buddhist Meditation. Reprinted by permission.

BODY IN THE MIRROR

My beautiful daughter, she is three, has formed a ritual around taking a bath. Every time she gets out of the tub, she will run to the full-length mirror and look at her body. Then she will throw up her arms, and yell, "I'M NAKED !!!!" and then run around the house, free and happy as a bird.

I began to realize her daily celebration of her body and thought, perhaps, I might try to do the same. I follow her now after every bath, and though I am only comfortable looking in the mirror with my underwear on, I am beginning to appreciate the body in the mirror.

Suzy, K.E.Y. Group member

CIRCLE OF STONES

How might it have been different for you, if, on your first menstrual day, your mother had given you a bouquet of flowers and taken you to lunch, and then the two of you had gone to meet your father at the jeweler, where your ears were pierced, and your father bought you your first pair of earrings, and then you went with a few of your friends and your mother's friends to get your first lip colouring;

> and then you went, for the very first time, to the Women's Lodge,
>
> to learn the wisdom of the women? How might your life be different?

Excerpted from *Circle of Stones*, by Judith Duerk. Page 9. Copyright © 1989 by LuraMedia.
Reprinted by permission of LuraMedia, Inc. San Diego, California.

How might your life have been different, if, through the years, there had been a place where you could go? . . . A place of women, away from the ordinary busy- ness of life . . . a place of women who knew the cycles of life, the ebb and flow of nature, who knew of times of work and times of quiet . . . who understood your tiredness and need for rest.

A place of women who could help you to accept your fatigue and trust your limitations, and to know, in the dark of winter, that your energy would return, as surely as the spring.

> Women who could help you learn to light a candle and to wait . . .
>
> How might your life be different?

Excerpted from *Circle of Stones*, by Judith Duerk. Page 60. Copyright © 1989 by LuraMedia.
Reprinted by permission of LuraMedia, Inc. San Diego, California.

BOUNDARIES

Purpose of Session:
1. Explore our boundaries in a creative way
2. Exploration and education of healthy boundaries
3. Share experiences and feelings and provide feedback to each other
4. Goal setting around boundaries

Time	Activity	Purpose
5 minutes	Centering Activity: "Rainbow Clouds" by Martha Belknap.	Assist members in becoming present centered.
15 minutes	Circle of Personal Power	Allow members to share thoughts and feelings.
5 minutes	Read: "Setting Boundaries" by Melody Beattie. Ask members to define "boundaries."	Direct attention to topic of boundaries and begin session on a common ground.
30 minutes	Activity: Boundary Breakers. Through a progression of personal questions, members will begin to develop ideas about each other. This activity serves to connect members as well as serve as a basis for processing what boundaries we set in disclosing information about ourselves. Option: at the end of the questions, ask members to share what ideas developed about the person to their right, or the group as a whole can comment on each member.	Through sharing, members link common experiences, emotions, and goals. Begin sharing on a deeper level, allowing members to offer feedback to each other to open barriers of how we are viewed by others.

20 minutes	Process: Depending on the questions you choose to ask during the activity, focus on consequences of boundaries, knowing when and how one is crossing a boundary, how it felt to be asked particular questions.	Bring the activity to a feeling level. Challenge members on their responses, boundaries, and ability to remain conscious during their decisions. Learn from others through sharing.
25 minutes	Discussion. Explore signs of healthy boundaries. Allow members to express what boundaries they have been successful at setting and what has enabled them to maintain them. Discuss tools and concrete ways people can begin to develop healthier boundaries.	Provide members with examples of healthy boundaries. Help them explore the connection between meeting their needs and the boundaries they set. Give them tools to work with.
5 minutes	Closure. Ask members to write three boundaries they would like to maintain and what they will need to do to be successful.	Set goals and focus on what is working for members, ask them to do more of that.

MATERIALS NEEDED:

Journals
Pens
Board or Pad
Chalk or Markers

RAINBOW CLOUDS

Purpose: quiet your breathing

Lie (or sit) down comfortably and close your eyes.

Imagine a clear blue summer sky overhead.
Notice some soft white fluffy clouds drifting by.
Invite one of those clouds to come visit you.

Watch it float down close to the ground.
Ride yourself inside of it.
Feel the cloud wrapped all around you.

Breathe in the softness of the cloud.
Watch the cloud become pink.
Breathe pink all around inside of you.

Notice how you are feeling.

Change the cloud to another color you like very much.
Breathe in your new color.

Notice how you are feeling now.

Change the color again. . . and again.
Breathe in all the colors you like the best.   (long pause)

Enjoy being wrapped in your rainbow.
Enjoy hiding inside your rainbow cloud.

From *Taming Your Dragons* by M. Belknap. Page 19. Reprinted by permission of
Martha Belknap, 1170 Dixon Road/Gold Hill, Boulder, CO 80302.

FLACK FROM SETTING BOUNDARIES

We need to know how far we'll go, and how far we'll allow others to go with us. Once we understand this, we can go anywhere.

- Beyond Codependency

When we own our power to take care of ourselves —set a boundary, say no, change an old pattern—we may get flack from some people. That's okay. We don't have to let their reactions control us, stop us, or influence our decision to take care of ourselves.

We don't have to control their reaction to our process of self-care. That is not our responsibility. We don't have to expect them not to react either.

People will react when we do things differently or take assertive action to nurture ourselves, particularly if our decision in some way affects them. Let them have their feelings. Let them have their reactions. But continue on your course anyway.

If people are used to us behaving in a certain way, they'll attempt to convince us to stay that way to avoid changing the system. If people are used to us saying yes all the time, they may start mumbling and murmuring when we say no. If people are used to us taking care of their responsibilities, feelings, and problems, they may give us some flack when we stop. That's normal. We can learn to live with a little flack in the name of healthy self-care.
Not abuse, mind you. Flack.

If people are used to controlling us through guilt, bullying, and badgering, they may intensify their efforts when we change and refuse to be controlled. That's okay. That's flack too.

We don't have to let flack pull us back into old ways if we've decided we want and need to change. We don't have to react to flack or give it much attention. It doesn't deserve it. It will die down.

Today, I will disregard any flack I receive for changing my behaviors or making other efforts to be myself.

Boundary Breakers

Instructions:

    A. Seat the group in a close circle on a padded floor.

    B. Each person must answer every question, with the proviso that she/he can pass in order to think. If a person passes twice, do not pressure her/him for an answer.

    C. Group members should not repeat the answer of someone else, if at all possible.

    D. Explanation of answers is not necessary and is, in fact, counter-productive to the flow and mood that you are trying to establish.

    E. Limit the size of the group or the number of questions so that the exercise does not become tedious.

Directions to Participants — Read the following to your group.

I'd like you to respond to a series of questions. Every answer you give is the correct one; no one will question your response or react to your answer in any way.

Please do not "cop out" by stealing someone else's answer. We will proceed around the circle, starting with a different person for each new question. If you can't think of an answer, you may PASS, and I'll come back to you.

Speak loudly so that everyone can hear. Be as honest as you can. Remember that we are interested in discovering good things about each other.

We are here as a group only to listen to each person's response. This is *not a debate*. We are not here to disagree, only to seek the person that is in each of us.

As each person answers, begin developing an idea of each person in the group and perhaps a few of the invisible boundaries, held by ignorance of one another, will begin to tumble.

Boundary-Breaking Questions

1) What is the best movie you have ever seen?

2) What is the most beautiful thing about people?

3) What is the ugliest thing you know?

4) What do you like to do most with a free afternoon?

5) On what basis do you select your acquaintances?

6) What is the greatest problem in the United States?

7) If you could smash one thing...what would you smash?

8) If you had one talent to choose, what would that one talent be?

9) What is the greatest value that guides your life?

10) What quality do you look for in a really good (friend) teacher?

11) Other than a relative, what one person has greatly influenced your life?

12) What gives you the most security?

13) What is the biggest waste you know of?

14) What is your greatest fear?

15) Select a word that you feel describes kids (people) of your age?

16) If you could give your principal (employer) one piece of advice...what would you tell him/her?

17) Name the most unreasonable thing that you know.

18) If you could choose to be a book...what book would you be?

19) If you were to paint a picture...what picture would you paint?

20) What do people like best about you?

21) What do you consider to be your biggest fault?

22) When do you feel most lonely?

23) What TV commercial bothers you the most?

24) What one thing would you change in your (life) school?

25) Describe your feelings about (fast food) chocolate .

26) Choose one word to describe (young) old people.

27) What future discovery are you looking forward to the most?

28) What subject is the most frequent topic of discussion among your peers?

29) If you could be a song, what song would you choose to be?

30) What is the very last thing that you will be willing to give up?

31) What is the best advice you have ever gotten?

32) When you are depressed, what cheers you up the most?

33) If you were tape recording the sound of violence...what sound would you use?

34) What is your least favorite food?

35) Describe the ideal family.

36) What is your favorite holiday?

37) What cartoon character do you identify with?

38) What scares you the most about next year?

BOUNDARY MESSAGES

CONFUSING MESSAGES	CONSEQUENCE	AFFIRMING BOUNDARY
Don't be selfish. Give to others first, even when it hurts.	I have no right to place my needs above others.	All people have needs and hopefully strive to fulfill them. Your needs are as important as mine, and we can compromise when there is conflict.
Help other people. Don't be demanding.	I have no right to make requests of other people.	You have a right to ask other people to change their behavior if their behavior affects your life. A request is not the same as a demand. If your rights are being violated and your requests are ignored, you have a right to make demands.
Be modest and humble. Don't act superior to others.	I have no right to do or share anything that would imply that I am better.	You have the right to show your ability and take pride in yourself. It is healthy to enjoy one's accomplishments.
Don't hurt other people's feelings.	I have no right to say what I really think or feel if it will hurt another person.	It is impossible to try to lead your life so as to never hurt someone. You have a right to express your thoughts and feelings. To deny others the opportunity to hear your truth is manipulative and phony. You are not responsible for how others react, you cannot keep people from their feelings. Your intention and goal in sharing feelings is important to consider.
Don't be a bitch. Don't complain.	I have no right to express or feel anger.	You have a right to your angry feelings. If you express them at the time they occur, they will not build and explode later on. It is important to express your anger assertively versus aggressively.
Watch my mood, body language facial expressions, and do as I want.	I must read the minds of others to figure out what they need.	I will tell you what I need, what I expect of you, and what my concerns are. You do not have to guess.

SIGNS OF UNHEALTHY BOUNDARIES

Awareness   Not noticing when someone invades your boundaries

Speaking   Revealing more than you feel comfortable with later
                         Speaking intimately on the first meeting
                         Fear of talking at all because you may say too much

Touching   Accepting food, gifts, touch, etc., that you don't want
                         Touching a person without asking

Expectations   Believing others can anticipate your needs
                         Falling apart so someone will take care of you

Personal Power   Letting others direct your life, make your choices, and
                         determine your identity

Relationships   Trusting too quickly in anyone who reaches out
                         Becoming preoccupied with someone
                         Adapting your behavior and values to please others

Sexuality   Being sexual when you don't want to
                         Being sexual for someone else, not self

Self-Care   All forms of self-abuse including addictions
                         Not stopping abuse done to you by others

DEFENDING OURSELVES

Purpose of Session:

1. Continue to build trust and cohesion among members
2. Self-exploration through experiential activities
3. Explore when we feel defensive and how we defend ourselves

Time	Activity	Purpose
5 minutes	Centering Activity: "A Shining Star" by Martha Belknap.	Assist members in becoming present centered.
15 minutes	Circle of Personal Power	Allow members to share immediate thoughts/feelings.
5 minutes	Activity: Ask members to write the word STRUGGLE vertically on a page in their journals. Next to each letter write a word or phrase that describes them.	Begin a progression of activities that grow in degree of risk and challenge. Use a tactile and visual activity metaphorically related to how we defend ourselves.
15 minutes	Process: Share. How much effort did members put into searching for accurate descriptions of themselves? How much of their day did they spend on automatic pilot? What are you doing when you're not on automatic pilot? Identify what happens when we get into "struggling" situations. When did you not struggle when you thought you would? What makes struggling easier?	Explore the need for members to share consciously, and get out of automatic pilot.

10 minutes	Activity: Cooperation Blanket. Lay a blanket out on the floor and ask members to stand on it. Ask the group if they would accept a more difficult challenge. Fold the blanket in half and present the challenge of trying to get all members on the blanket (bearing one's own weight for safety reasons), until the group decides, as a whole, to stop.	Continue the progression with an activity requiring communication, touch, and problem solving.
15 minutes	Process: What factors contributed to the group's success? What, if anything, was uncomfortable for individuals during the activity? How did they alleviate the discomfort? How was the decision made to stop?	Explore what the group did well and what individuals did when they felt discomfort.
5 minutes	Activity: With a rope or other boundary marker, form a circle on the floor. Ask members to stand outside of the circle and choose a partner they preferably do not know well. When each person is ready they may step into the circle and face their partner, at which time the challenge is simply to stare into each others eyes. When an individual becomes uncomfortable, ask them to step outside of the circle. (Blinking is okay. This is a silent activity.) Ask members to think about how they responded to that challenge. Ask them to switch partners and repeat the activity, this time trying to maintain eye contact through the discomfort in an effort to work through it and understand it.	End the progression of activities with an intimate activity that challenges members to become aware of how they are defending themselves and clarifies what it is they are defending themselves from.

20 minutes	Process: What was it like for you to experience this activity? How many of you can identify with the experience of being in the store and choosing to look at the floor instead of another human being? What are we defending ourselves from? How did you defend yourself in this activity? What are some exceptions? What is the opposite of defending? Share (from the following information) some of the defenses we tend to use to protect our core feelings. Ask members to share what those feelings might be and why they need protection.	Bring the group deeper by challenging them to be conscious of how they are defending themselves.
5 minutes	Closure. Journal the ways we can advocate for ourselves and what we are willing to do when we feel these feelings or defenses.	Ask members to become aware of their feelings and behaviors.

MATERIALS NEEDED:

Journals/Pens
Blanket or Tarp
Rope or other boundary marker

Photo by Pat Athey

A Shining Star

Purpose: feel strong and rested

Sit comfortably and close your eyes.
Imagine the dark sky at night.
Look up at the bright stars.
See the word STAR in your mind.
Imagine the letters S-T-A-R on the inside of your eyelids.
As you look at the letter S, breathe in **strength.**
Feel strength inside your body.
As you look at the letter T, breathe in **trust.**
Feel trust inside your heart.
As you look at the letter A, breathe in **awareness.**
Feel awareness inside your mind.
As you look at the letter R, breathe in **rest.**
Feel rest inside your whole self.

Now picture a beautiful bright shining star.
Feel the peace of the night sky.
Let your own star be very special for you.
See how brightly it shines!

From *Taming Your Dragons* by M. Belknap. Page 13. Reprinted by permission of
Martha Belknap, 1170 Dixon Road/Gold Hill, Boulder, CO 80302.

DEFENSES

Most of us have rules or guidelines for how to control or manage our lives. These rules or guidelines help us get out of uncomfortable situations. We may make a joke, or become angry, isolated, or intellectualized. When the discomfort is relieved through humor or anger, or rationalizing the situation, the behavior is reinforced, and we continue to use it in other difficult situations. As a result, we tend to rely on this pattern or defense automatically in uncomfortable situations. The problem arises when this pattern is not as useful anymore, yet we still cling to it. People learn to develop defense mechanisms as a protection against their own anxiety.

We protect our core feelings of:

fear	**rejection**
inadequacy	**embarrassment**
loneliness	**helplessness**
hurt	**vulnerability**

With defenses such as:

denial	**being super responsible**
anger	**humor**
perfectionism	**intellectualizing**
aggression	**charm**
control	**blaming**

When the wall of defenses can be shaken, even momentarily, some deep feelings might be experienced. Some emotions can be very intense. and without our normal defenses intact, we are given an opportuninty to experience new feelings and new ways of reacting.

Feelings will intensify when we get closer to unknown territory. Feeling anxiety, fear, excitement, and confusion is both normal and predictable. Physiological symptoms may persist such as a racing heart, sweaty palms, nervous stomach, or weakness in the knees. Stepping outside of our normal range of comfort creates these feelings. Feelings are not things to be feared, yet we spend an enormous amount of time trying to remain comfortable.

Challenge yourself to become aware when you experience different feelings, and even more aware of how you respond when you feel that way. Learn to feel your feelings. They are a gauge to be conscious of, rather than a flashing red light that means DANGER and STOP.

DEPRESSION AS AN OPPORTUNITY FOR GROWTH

Purpose of Session:
1. Self-exploration around characteristics and frequency of depression
2. Recognize familiar sensations, self-talk, emotions, and behavior patterns associated with one's own depression
3. Distinguish between clinical depression and day-to-day mild depression
4. Discover tools to combat depression

Time	Activity	Purpose
5 minutes	Centering Activity: Stretching Lead the group, or ask for a volunteer to present some stretches to loosen members up.	Bring group to the here and now.
15 minutes	Circle of Personal Power	Allow members to share thoughts and/or feelings.
10 minutes	Written exercise in Journal: Define what depression means to you What are the familiar and predictable things you experience when depressed (i.e., sensations, self-talk, emotions, behaviors)? What percentage of this past week have you spent in depression? Past month?	Begin to focus members on session's topic and own it. Begin to show predictable patterns involved in depression.
40 minutes	Differentiate between signs of clinical depression vs. mild, daily depression. This session focuses on mild depression. Discuss written exercises and information sheets exploring sensations, self-talk, emotions, and behaviors familiar to members. Exploration of what leads us toward and away from depression.	Bring members deeper by asking them to share with others while becoming aware of their own process of "depressing."

5 minutes	Activity: More stretching.	A physical activity to ground members and increase energy level. Role models a tool for depression.
5 minutes	Closure: What will you take with you from today's session?	Allow members to express what the session has brought to their awareness and how they will use the information in their lives.

MATERIALS NEEDED:

Journals

Pens

Visual effects may include: black balloons around the room

cake with black frosting (depression party)

Typical Symptoms of Depression

The following descriptions are representative of what may be seen in mildly, moderately, and severely depressed people. It is not necessary for all the characteristics in any one category to be present; the degree and frequency may be a better gauge. These following characteristics are not complete, but seek to provide a guideline in understanding the different degrees of depression.

MILD DEPRESSION

Mild depression typically fluctuates during the day and may be relieved by outside events such as jokes or compliments. A common feeling is sadness and often disappointment in one's self. Somewhat withdrawn, mildly depressed people may prefer passive activities, such as watching television, and will postpone other activities that take more energy. They may feel less intense love and affection and there is an increased tendency to cry, particularly in women. Cognitively, mildly depressed people tend to internalize errors or difficulties as if they reflect personal inadequacy. Self-blame and criticism is high and feelings of inferiority and indecisiveness are common. Physically, mildly depressed people may experience a loss or gain of weight, sleep disturbances, and they may tire more easily. There may be a slight loss of spontaneous sexual desire and responsiveness. Such people may express a desire to be dead. These desires are often passive and there is no wish to do anything active to kill themselves. Mild depression is usually a response to a loss or disappointment in life.

MODERATE DEPRESSION

Experiencing a more intense and persistent sadness, moderately depressed individuals are more difficult to cheer up and any relief is temporary. The feelings tend to be stronger in the mornings and their feelings of dislike for themselves may turn to disgust. There is a general feeling of boredom, and these people may come to feel indifferent and cut themselves off from others. Moderately depressed people may feel powerless and frightened about what is happening to them. Their thoughts tend to focus on their deficiencies and past failures and they feel little hope. The risk for either planned or impulsive suicide is high, and sleep patterns become erratic. Sometimes they may wake after 3 or 4 hours, other times they may sleep for 12 hours. Constantly tired, any activity seems to make them more tired.

SEVERE DEPRESSION

The constant sadness and hopelessness that severely depressed people feel is very painful. They come to hate themselves and feel no enjoyment in life. Relations with others are characterized by apathy and negative feelings, and they often feel they are a burden to others.

Cognitively, severely depressed people see themselves as worthless and totally incompetent. Experiencing extreme self-blame and criticism, such individuals feel a total paralysis of the will and seek seclusion in bed, in the dark, or in killing themselves. Suicidal wishes are prevalent, but typically, they do not have enough energy to carry out the act. Physically, eating and sleeping diminish to the point to where they lose a considerable amount of weight and they may feel as though they lie awake thinking all night. There is a total aversion to sex and anything requiring energy.

Adapted from *The Diagnosis and Management of Depression*
by A. T. Beck, M.D. Copyright 1973 by University of Pennsylvania Press.

DEPRESSION AS AN OPPORTUNITY FOR GROWTH

Depression, like anything else in life, can be received as a gift that can aid you in your spiritual growth. If you are willing to find compassion for yourself in the midst of the dull pain of depression, you will, perhaps, see this is so. Depression may be your best opportunity to see how you cause yourself to suffer, to accept that process, to embrace yourself, and to let go in compassion and end the suffering.

Each time you are depressed, stop and turn your attention inward. Imagine that you are someone you have no reason to dislike. Pay attention to all your feelings and begin to write them down. No analysis, just allow it to come out like a volcano. Express it in whatever way. The point? When you do this kind of process, you will begin to see patterns. You will begin to see the steps you take that lead to self-rejection and depression. You will notice your fears and assumptions and conditioned reactions to circumstances. It will begin to become clear that depression is something YOU DO, not some larger-than-life ogre to which you are victim.

Your depression is not random.

You feel, think, say and believe the same things every time. Perhaps **what** you are depressing changes. **How** you depress remains the same. The only way we can know what is going on is to sit down with an open mind and pay attention. If we watch closely enough, we notice that there are **SENSATIONS** in our bodies that go with depression. They don't vary. They're the same every time. We label this one depression. With this label comes a learned response, the **SELF-TALK**—everything we've been taught to believe about depression. What it is, what it means, what I am for feeling it, what will happen as a result, and how the future will be.

When the talk starts, we have an **EMOTIONAL REACTION** to it.
> I don't want this.
> I am afraid.
> This is too painful.
> Oh no, not this again.

And then comes a conditioned **BEHAVIOR PATTERN** which is usually avoidance or escape.
> I should quit my job.
> I've got to leave town.
> I need a drink (or drug).

> I want a divorce.
> I'm going to kill myself.
> I can't function. (paralysis)

From *The Depression Book. Depression as an Opportunity for Growth.* Pages 1-9.
Copyright 1991 by A Center for Zen Buddhist Meditation. Reprinted by permission.

The sequence is :   SENSATION
                         SELF-TALK
                         EMOTION
                         BEHAVIOR PATTERN

THESE ARE GOING ON ALL THE TIME, NOT JUST IN DEPRESSION.

Trying to figure out in our heads why we are feeling a certain way just takes us farther and farther away from ourselves. Give yourself permission to feel whatever you feel instead of having standards about how you should be. It is not true that certain feelings are okay and others are not. "Okay" and "not okay" are thoughts. When we put thoughts in charge of feelings we get into trouble. It's not the feeling we're having that's a problem, it's our judgment about that feeling.

Our feelings are the most intimate experience we have of ourselves.

Very often we think we need to blame ourselves for our feelings, or feel guilt about them, and then punish or discipline ourselves. But really, what we do about our feelings determines the quality of our relationship with ourselves.

If we can create a safe, loving place within ourselves for how we feel, then we can create it for all aspects of who we are. How can you be with your depression as though you were being with one of your children who came to you and said, "Mom, I'm depressed"? You wouldn't say, "Get out of here. I don't want to hear that kind of talk." The work is to develop the same relationship with yourself that you would be willing to have with someone you love.

DEPRESSION...

        brings me back to myself in a way much of life does not. It gets my attention. It brings me to a halt. It says, "Stop! Pay Attention!", which I am usually not willing to do for myself. It is life's way of keeping all our emotions from happening at once.

Depression can actually be a way of taking care of ourselves. It can be protection, solace, comfort. We can view it like a soft blanket we can wrap up in. It's no accident that when people get depressed they often go to bed and eat. We attempt to return to a sort of infant state. We reduce the world to a simple sleep and eat state. This slows us down and gives us time to find the line between denying ourselves and indulging ourselves. It helps us discover what we really need.

BIG QUESTION:

HOW MUCH OF THE PROBLEM IS WITH THE WAY I ACTUALLY FEEL, AND HOW MUCH IS WITH WHAT I'M TELLING MYSELF ABOUT HOW I FEEL?

One of the most commonly depressed emotions is anger. When we are children, anger is frightening because it is so unacceptable to adults. We often turn this anger inward against ourselves. As adults, we react with: guilt, fear, self-hate, illness, aggression, (fill in the blank_____). We want to treat emotions like house guests. If we give them the master bedroom with the hot tub, and TV, they're never going to leave. But if we throw a sleeping bag on the floor of the garage, they won't feel welcome. We want to find a place in-between where they feel welcome but know they're not invited to stay forever. An emotion that feels rejected gets stronger. It becomes like a dog that you don't feed enough or a child who doesn't get enough attention.

WHAT WE RESIST, PERSISTS.

Learn to express emotions *to yourself*. It is always safe to express how you feel to yourself. We think we have to keep our feelings dammed up or else there will be a flood. But if we never dammed them up, a flood would be much less likely!

ALL YOU HAVE TO DO IS ACKNOWLEDGE HOW YOU ARE FEELING AND THEN TREAT YOURSELF AS YOU WOULD TREAT A FRIEND WHO WAS FEELING THE SAME WAY.

If we're going to find out who we are, we have to stop beating on ourselves long enough to open up to ourselves in order to find out who we are.

ACCEPTANCE

The first step is always acceptance. Each time we grasp our willingness to see these things, without judgment, we take one step closer to freedom.

The only thing that gives these negative feelings any power is our fear of them.

LEADS TOWARD DEPRESSION:

> Raising your standards until you're dissatisfied
>
> Not doing what gives your life meaning
>
> Repressing how you are and with that, depressing the life you know
> you could be living

LEADS AWAY FROM DEPRESSION:

> Being present
>
> Not trying to change anything
>
> Accepting what is

HOW DO YOU BEGIN TO UNCOVER WHAT'S UNDER THE DEPRESSION?

You GET IT that there's a GOOD REASON for being depressed and ACCEPT that it's OKAY to feel that way. "I won't SEE what's going on with me because I BELIEVE there is something wrong with it ('I'm depressed, there's something wrong with me')."

> JUST FOR A LITTLE WHILE BE OPEN TO THE POSSIBILITY THAT
> THERE IS NOTHING WRONG WITH YOU.

Projecting into the future from a present depression causes me to see a depressing future.... I believe that what I'm experiencing is real. If I let go of that and get into the present, I realize the present is quite manageable. The feeling is only a feeling—the label is upsetting.

> HOW I TREAT MYSELF IN DEPRESSION IS MORE IMPORTANT
> THAN GETTING OVER IT OR WHAT I'LL DO WHEN IT'S OVER.

When I stop depressing the feelings, I can begin to take care of the parts of me who feel isolated, vulnerable and afraid. If I stay in the depression, I'll never see what is underneath it. Being depressed and unhappy sometimes is just part of life. It doesn't mean that something has gone wrong with life any more than rain is something that has gone wrong with the weather or night is something that has gone wrong with the day.

The difference between allowing yourself to feel real pain or depressing that pain is the difference between being cut by a knife or enveloped by fog. The cut will heal, usually quicker than you think, and life can go on. But you can live your whole life in the fog, buffered against the experience of pain. The sadness is that when protected from pain we are also protected from joy.

From *The Depression Book. Depression as an Opportunity for Growth.* Pages 69, 73-75, 81-83, 89-90, 96. Copyright 1991 by A Center for Zen Buddhist Meditation. Reprinted by permission.

LIVING YOUR LIFE IN FEAR THAT YOU'RE GOING TO DO IT WRONG
IS LIKE AN EXPLORER WHO IS AFRAID OF GETTING LOST.

Depression can happen when we try not to be unhappy. We want to go from one peak to the next without traveling through the valleys below.

Peaks/Valleys   Up/Down   Right/Wrong

**One cannot exist without the other.
Feeling guilty over being who you are does nothing but rob you of your life.**

We have our identity in this process of depressing. We are afraid that if we stop, we won't know how to be, won't know who to be, won't know what life will expect. It is safer and more comfortable to continue with the depressing than to risk the freedom.

It is okay to change. It is okay to try something new. Because if you try and don't like it, you can always return to how you were doing it before. And not taking a risk because you are afraid is a grave disservice to yourself. Fear is not the problem. You can have your fear and allow it to stop you, or you can have your fear and risk anyway. Either way, the fear is there.

THE CHOICE IS YOURS.

EMPOWERMENT

Purpose of Session:
1. Define and explore our "power" and ways to nurture our power
2. Recognize, through an experiential activity, how we give our power away
3. Create our own affirmations to support our power and self-worth

Time	Activity	Purpose
5 minutes	Centering Activity: "Creating Your Special Place"	Assist members in becoming present centered.
15 minutes	Circle of Personal Power	Allow members to share immediate thoughts and feelings.
20 minutes	Explore "our power" and what about it is powerful. List ideas on the board. (Examples are on the following page)	Explore the power within us, giving credit and worth to our skills and inner self.
15 minutes	Activity: Group Juggle (Facilitation guide on following page)	Use of experiential activity as a metaphor for how we lose our power in the midst of chaos, and how to maintain our focus on our powers.
25 minutes	Process: How are the objects used similar to your powers? What is happening in your life when you drop the "ball"? What is the feeling? What distracts you from your power?	Allow members to explore metaphorically how they view their "power over the

What did you learn in this juggle in order to gain control over the group juggle? What have you learned in your life that enables you to maintain your power in chaos?

pattern" of juggling. Share insights on tools to maintain our power and feelings that emerge when we give our power away.

5 minutes

Share how affirmations work and how to enter positive thoughts in our minds. A tool to maintain our power, is making our mind believe we have it.

Sharing a tool of affirmation to release positive thoughts into our chatterbox that can sometimes sabotage our feeling of power.

5 minutes

Closing. Give each member one of the power balls used in the exercise. Ask members what power they would like to maintain or give attention to this week and what tools will they use to do that.

Expressing what was experienced and how to maintain our power.

MATERIALS NEEDED:

Board and chalk (Pad and pens)
Variety of balls or inanimate objects—Keep safety in mind
(Helpful metaphors are wooden hearts, rubber eggs, koosh balls, etc.)
Journals and pens

DIRECTIONS FOR THE GROUP JUGGLE:

Assemble the group into a circle. Begin with a ball (koosh ball, tennis ball, etc.), metaphorically framing the similarities between the ball and a power listed earlier on the board. By throwing the balls underhand (for safety) and trying not to throw to someone next to them, each member will receive the ball once, forming a pattern that will initiate the group juggle. Ask members to remember who they threw it to and who they got it from. Ask the members, when they receive the ball, to identify one of their strongest powers. Then, once they have thrown the ball, ask them to cross their arms so members know who has not yet had the ball.

Once the pattern is established, begin to add more balls. Add enough balls until there is chaos, as when we move too fast in life and lose focus of the present moment, we sometimes experience chaos. Gather the balls back into your bag and ask members to describe that experience. Relate their expressions back to power and how the activity can be representative of giving our power away.

What skills or tools can aid them in maintaining the focus? Repeat the activity and process the difference. This time around add a rubber egg, or some other surprise, to highlight how once we think we have it figured out, life throws us another surprise. Owning our power during chaos is crucial.

Ask members to sit and allow them to hold on to one of the objects to continue the kinesthetic experience of feeling a power. Begin to process the significant points of the activity. Identify tools, feelings, and support systems. To conclude the processing circle, utilize each ball as a personal goal members make by tossing their ball into the circle.

Adapted from Silver Bullets by K. Rohnke. Page 112.
Copyright 1984 by Kendall/Hunt Publishing Company.

Photo by Tim Athey

CREATING YOUR SPECIAL PLACE

In creating your own special place you will be making a retreat for relaxation and guidance. This place may be indoors or out. In structuring your place, follow a few guidelines:
*   Allow a private entry into your place.
*   Make it peaceful, comfortable and safe.
*   Fill your place with sensuous detail. Create a midground, a foreground, and a background.
*   Allow room for an inner guide or other person to comfortably be with you.

To go to your safe place, lie down, be totally comfortable. Close your eyes . . . Walk slowly to a quiet place in your mind . . . Your place can be inside or outside . . . It needs to be peaceful and safe . . . Picture yourself unloading your anxieties, your worries . . . Notice the view in the distance. . . What do you smell? . . . What do you hear? . . . Notice what it is before you . . . Reach out and touch it . . . How does it feel? . . . Smell it . . . Hear it . . . Make the temperature comfortable . . . Be safe here . . . Look around for a special spot, a private spot . . . Find the path to this place . . . Feel the ground with your feet . . . Look above you . . . What do you see? . . . Hear? . . . Smell? . . . Walk down this path until you can enter your own quiet, comfortable, safe place.

You have arrived at your special place . . . What is under your feet? . . . How does it feel? . . . Take several steps . . . What do you see above you? . . . What do you hear? . . . Do you hear something else? . . . Reach and touch something . . . What is its texture? . . . Are there pens, paper, paints nearby, or is there sand to draw in, clay to work? . . . Go to them, handle them, smell them. These are your special tools, or tools for your inner guide to reveal ideas or feelings to you . . . Look as far as you can see . . . What do you see? . . . What do you hear? . . . What aromas do you notice?

Now you need to find a place for your inner guide and a path from which your guide can enter. Sit or lie in your special place . . . Notice its smells, sounds, sights . . . This is your place and nothing can harm you here . . . If danger is here, expel it . . . Spend three to five minutes realizing you are relaxed, safe and comfortable.

Memorize this place's smells, tastes, sights, sounds . . . You can come back and relax here whenever you want . . . Leave by the same path or entrance . . . Notice the ground, touch things near you . . . Look far away and appreciate the view . . . Remind yourself this special place you created can be entered whenever you wish. Say an affirmation such as, "I can relax here," or "This is my special place. I can come here whenever I wish."

Now open your eyes and spend a few seconds appreciating your relaxation.

From *The Relaxation and Stress Reduction Workbook*, by M. Davis and E. Eshelman. Pages 59-60.
Published by New Harbinger Publications. Reprinted by permission.

KEEPING OUR POWER

DEFINE POWER (Power over self, not others):

Knowledge is power
Support vs. isolation
Asking for what we need
ACTION is power
Following our intuition
Trusting our choices
Being a woman
Setting boundaries
Having a positive chatterbox
Spirituality
Speaking your truth
Seeking resolution to conflicts
Feeling your feelings and not judging them
Taking responsibility for your choices, feelings, behaviors
Taking responsibility for your life
Using "I" statements
Self-care
Being honest with self and others
Humor
Being able to be alone with yourself
Living life consciously vs. on automatic pilot
Being clear on what you feel...and what you need.
Acknowledging the worth in self and others
Solution- vs. problem-focused approach to life
Practicing detachment when appropriate
Affirming your past...and living in the moment
Responding vs. reacting to situations
Moving through the fear
The simple words, "I can handle it."
UNCONDITIONAL SELF-LOVE is the greatest power of all

Identifying the feeling that accompanies giving our power away is essential in recognizing when we are playing the victim role and gives us the awareness that we can take responsibility for making changes in some way. Keeping your power can be difficult at first. Similar to setting boundaries, people do not want us to change our ways, or speak our truth. Seek the approval of yourself first. Remember, security is not having things, it's handling things.

IDENTIFY WHEN YOU GIVE YOUR POWER AWAY, AND THE FEELINGS THAT ACCOMPANY IT:

POWER	FEELING
Taking the responsibility or blame for another person	Feel like a victim
Allowing the negative chatterbox to continue	Worthless
Not expressing your truth	Powerless
Choosing to stay stuck in fear...anger...pain	Hopeless/powerless
Letting others make choices for you	Powerless

IDENTIFY TOOLS TO SUPPORT YOU IN KEEPING YOUR POWER:

Ask for support from others

Slow down—become aware of your feelings and body posture

BE CONSCIOUS!

Breathe

Respond vs. react

Practice "I" statements like "I feel" and "I need" regularly so they become the norm for you

Practice self-love

Choose to surround yourself with positive healthy people who accept you

Set boundaries

Make choices and accept the consequences

AFFIRMATIONS

Affirmations are positive messages you give yourself, preferably written and verbal. We have negative messages or tapes playing in our minds which affect our behavior. In order to eliminate these negative messages, we can consciously replace them with positive messages, which can produce permanent desirable changes in our lives.

1. Work with one or more every day. The best times are just before sleeping, before starting the day, and when you are feeling down.

2. Write each affirmation ten or twenty times.

3. Write in first person, own the affirmation.

4. Continue working with the affirmations daily until they become totally integrated into your consciousness. You will know this when your mind responds positively, and when you begin to experience the intended results.

5. Record your affirmations on cassette tapes and play them back when you can. If you fall asleep while the earphone is still in your ear and the tape is going, the autosuggestion is still working as you sleep.

6. It is effective to look into the mirror and say the affirmations to yourself out loud. Keep saying them until you are able to see yourself with a relaxed, happy expression. Keep saying them until you eliminate all facial tension and grimaces.

7. Hanging sticky notes on the refrigerator, rearview mirror, bathroom, and other commonly used areas can increase your exposure to a positive chatterbox.

8. As we work with affirmations, we gradually become aware of the people, situations, and attitudes of mind that foster healthy qualities.

To create your own affirmations, think of the qualities you wish to affirm in yourself. Then state these qualities as simply as possible. Always state them in the present tense. In that way, the unconscious mind understands the goal and will work to bring it about. Say, "I am strong, energetic, and competent" rather than "I am going to grow strong, energetic, and competent." The latter puts the situation in the future and the mind won't respond to it.

YOUR POWER IS ALWAYS IN THE PRESENT.

SOME POSITIVE AFFIRMATIONS:

I am a strong, centered, and creative woman/man.

I am in charge of my life and am making conscious choices.

I have a lot to offer anyone in a relationship.

I deserve to be loved the way I want to be loved.

I am able to deal with my anger openly, honestly, and appropriately.

I am able to see where I need to direct my energies.

I am healthy, wise, and loving of myself and others.

I have a body. I am more than my body. I have a mind. I am more than my mind. I have emotions. I am more than my emotions.

I love myself; I am patient and gentle with myself.

I am where I am supposed to be.

I am able to release all tensions and resentments.

I intuitively eat the amount and kind of food necessary to nourish and sustain me.

I am honest, open, and direct in my communication with others.

I have the energy, courage, and resources to make those changes I need to make.

I use my anger as an agent of transformation.

I am reaching deep within the source of my creativity.

COURAGE: THE POWER TO LET GO OF THE FAMILIAR.
Ray Lindquist

EXPRESSING FEELINGS

Purpose of Session:
1. Explore feelings and emotions through drawing
2. Increase our vocabulary of "feeling" words
3. Explore what happens when we don't express our feelings
4. Learn to communicate through I-statements
5. Practicing I-statements to be used in the immediate future

Time	Activity	Purpose
5 minutes	Centering Activity: "What Can You Hear" by Martha Belknap.	Assist members in becoming present centered.
15 minutes	Circle of Personal Power	Allow members to share immediate thoughts and feelings.
15 minutes	Activity: Drawing and Smearing Ask members to think of a current situation in their lives that has evoked emotion. Ask them to draw those emotions.	Use of an experiential activity to express feelings and emotions.
20 minutes	Process: Share drawings and emotions. Ask members how they have coped with those emotions and what they need from others in order to express them.	Begin sharing personal experiences around emotion and understanding what we need when we feel emotion.
25 minutes	Share tools for expressing emotions constructively (I-statements). Identify different emotions to increase one's vocabulary. Explore what happens to unexpressed emotions.	Offer tools to members as a way to increase choices and awareness.

10 minutes	Closing. Relate back to the pictures the members drew. Ask them to construct an I-statement they may use regarding that situation in the near future.	Allow setting of goals for members to concretely use what they have learned. Provide feedback on this new skill.

MATERIALS NEEDED:

      Markers/Crayons or chalk
      Drawing paper
      Paper towels (when using chalk)
      Journals

What Can You Hear?

Purpose: self-awareness

Lie down comfortably and close your eyes.
Say your own name quietly to yourself.
Hear your name echo softly inside your head.
Pretend that you can hear your hair growing.

Listen to your breathing.   (long pause)
Hear the breath at the back of your throat.
Listen to your heartbeat.   (long pause)
Hear the blood flowing like a tiny stream.

Feel your chest moving as you breathe. (long pause)
Hear the air as it leaves your lungs.
Imagine that you can listen inside from the back of your belly button.
What sounds can you hear?   (long pause)

Imagine that you can listen outside with the tips of your fingers.
What sounds can you bring back into your hands?   (long pause)
Imagine that you can pick up sounds with the bottom of your toes.
How do your feet feel? (long pause)

Pretend that you can hear your toenails growing.
Pretend that you can listen to the world around you through the holes of your skin.
What can you hear now?

From *Taming Your Dragons* by M. Belknap. Page 38. Reprinted by permission of
Martha Belknap, 1170 Dixon Road/Gold Hill, Boulder, CO 80302.

EXPRESSION OF FEELINGS

People frequently have a misunderstanding about the way litter biodegrades in the wilderness. This misconception also applies to how we deal with feelings. Many people believe that if painful and uncomfortable feelings are left unattended, they will magically disappear. "It's biodegradable" is a common response to asking why someone threw an orange peel on the ground. It seems there is a magical quality given to the term biodegradable which indicates something will dissolve or decompose. What is often misunderstood is the time or duration involved in this deterioration process. During this process, the substance is a contaminate that alters the ecology. Examples include:

aluminum cans:	80-100 years to decompose
paper containers with plastic coating:	5 years
orange peels:	1 week to 6 months

In a similar manner, unresolved feelings are a contaminate to the human system. Even though feelings are hidden or repressed, individuals are influenced or even imprisoned by them. The impact of these feelings usually occurs unconsciously and people are not aware of them at work inside the body. Because feelings are hidden we often think that others won't see them. Yet we've all met people about whom we later wonder, "What is he so mad about?" or " What's her problem?"

When you bury a feeling, you bury it alive. It may grow in unexpected and unwanted ways.

WHAT TO DO WITH FEELINGS:

1. **Identify and acknowledge feelings**

2. **Experience them and accept them for what they are**
   Accept and own feelings as being a valuable component of being human. It's okay to feel emotions, even if they don't feel good.
   In an effort to honor your feelings, avoid spending time trying to explain them, find a reason for them, or search for their cause.

3. **Share them with someone you trust**
   A common fear is once I start, I won't be able to stop. Feelings act like waves, with moments of intensity and calmness. When feelings are truly felt and experienced, there is a shift. A release. A freedom from the imprisonment.

LET IT OUT—LET OTHERS IN—LET IT GO.

SOME FEELING WORDS

contented	angry	disappointed
comfortable	embarrassed	disgusted
joyful	frightened	frustrated
close	shy	grouchy
warm	annoyed	confused
grateful	depressed	hurt
thankful	guilty	impatient
cheerful	anxious	insecure
loving	nervous	jealous
excited	despairing	resentful
confident	enraged	stubborn
hopeful	terrified	upset
proud	worried	worthless
respectful	ashamed	concerned
satisfied	desperate	discouraged
secure	offended	defiant
in pain	shocked	fearful
cold	threatened	nervous

USING I-STATEMENTS

When we send "You" messages to people—"You make me angry," "You don't listen to me"—they may feel embarrassed, angry, hurt, or insulted. "You" messages shift the focus of the feelings to the other person, and result in blaming, accusing, or labeling other people. "You" messages often don't work because when we blame others for our feelings, we risk them not accepting the blame.

When we express our feelings and concerns in "I" messages, we take responsibility for ourselves and communicate openly, clear and direct. We are asking for their help. We say, "I'm worried," "I'm concerned," "I'm afraid," "I'm disappointed," and we tell why. We take responsibility for our own feelings and leave the person's behavior up to them. "I" messages avoid the negative impact that accompanies "You" messages, freeing the person to be considerate and helpful, rather than resentful, angry, and defensive.

CONSTRUCTING I-MESSAGES

"I" messages focus on an individual's feelings and on other people's behaviors, not on people themselves. You are upset with a particular act, not with the total individual. "I" messages begin with "when" and separate the deed from the doer: "When people interrupt each other...," "When I see you with my ex-husband...." The action that you describe is usually not the real reason for your concern but rather a consequence of the behavior. "Because" is used to connect the feelings with the consequences.

1. **Description of the behavior:**
   "When we talk about our problems with each other..."

2. **Statement of your feelings regarding the possible consequences of the behavior.**
   "...I get defensive..."

3. **State what those consequences are or might be.**
   "...because I feel misunderstood."

   "When we sit in silence during arguments, I become afraid, fearing we won't resolve our differences."

4. **Sometimes the feelings may be eliminated:**

"When we don't listen to each other, I stop talking."

"When my job becomes stressful, I lose my focus."

"When you come home late without calling, I become worried."

5. **Sometimes "you" is used when it is descriptive and not critical or blaming:**

"When you are late coming home from school, I worry something may have happened to you."

6. **Using "I Feel and I Need" communicates the next step for response.**

"I feel disappointed when I see you call your sister names, and I need you to be respectful to her."

"When you disapprove of my friends, I feel defensive. I need you to trust my judgment."

"I feel angry when your love is conditional, and I need you to be honest with me about your feelings."

"I feel ignored when you do not respond to my questions, and I need you to acknowledge my presence."

FEAR

Purpose of Session:
1. Self-exploration of our personal fears
2. Gain insight on what keeps us stuck in our fears
3. Discover tools to assist members in overcoming fears

Time	Activity	Purpose
5 minutes	Centering Activity: "You Are the Ocean" by Martha Belknap	Focus group and bring them to the here and now.
15 minutes	Circle of Personal Power	Allow members to share thoughts and feelings.
5 minutes	Written exercise: Journal five fears you are currently experiencing in your life today. Define what fear means for you.	Begin to focus members on the session's topic and create a personal connection with fear.
10 minutes	Present the first 2 levels of fear, as illustrated in *Feel the Fear and Do It Anyway*, by Susan Jeffers, and ask members to write down what they feel might be the underlying feeling in each of their fears.	Bring the group to a deeper level by asking members to ponder the underlying feelings associated with fear.
15 minutes	Discussion. Allow members to give feedback to those experiencing confusion on what they feel an underlying feeling may be.	Help members identify internal vs. external fears and allow expression of those feelings.
30 minutes	Continue discussion, shifting the focus of the Level 3 fear, "I can't handle it," to tools used to move from a position of pain to a position of power. Address vocabulary, our chatterbox, reclaiming our power, and affirmations.	Begin to give members tools to move beyond their fears. Acknowledge and validate physical and emotional fears.

| 10 minutes | Closing. Journal: Specific tools to challenge our fears? What fears have you handled recently? List them. What contributed to your success? | Reaffirm tools for handling our fears, and process what members experienced today. |

MATERIALS NEEDED:

Journals/Pens

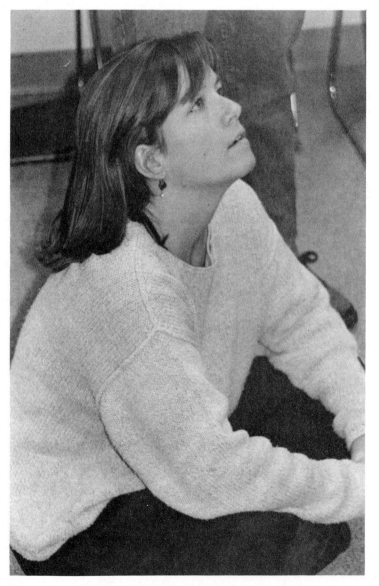

Photo by Tim Athey

YOU ARE THE OCEAN

Purpose: listen to your breathing

Sit comfortably and close your eyes.

Let go of your cheeks and jaw.

Let go of your shoulders and elbows.

Imagine that you are at the beach in the summertime.

(Long pause)

Feel the warm sunshine on your face.

Smell the salt air.

Taste the salt on your lips.

Feel the cool ocean breeze on your skin.

Listen to the sound of your breathing.

(Long pause)

As you breathe in, see the waves roll in.

As you breathe out, hear the waves roll out.

Feel your breath flowing with the ocean.

Feel the rhythm of the waves.

Let the sunshine soak into your body.

Be at peace with the waves.

Be at peace with your breathing.

Become one with the ocean.

From *Taming Your Dragons* by M. Belknap. Page 34. Reprinted by permission of
Martha Belknap, 1170 Dixon Road/Gold Hill, Boulder, CO 80302.

FEAR

LEVEL 1 FEARS (Exterior situations)

<u>Those That Happen</u>

aging

becoming disabled

retirement

being alone

children leaving home

natural disasters

loss of financial security

change

dying

war

illness

accidents

rape

losing a loved one

<u>Those Requiring Action</u>

going back to school

making decisions

changing a career

making friends

ending or beginning a relationship

using the telephone

asserting oneself

losing weight

being interviewed

making a mistake

driving

public speaking

intimacy

LEVEL 2 FEARS (Inner states of mind that reflect your sense of self and your ability to handle this world)

rejection

success

failure

being vulnerable

being conned

helplessness

disapproval

loss of image

LEVEL 3 FEARS (The fear that keeps you stuck)

I CAN'T HANDLE IT

At the bottom of every one of your fears is simply the fear that you can't handle whatever life may bring you. If you knew you could handle anything that came your way, what would you possibly have to fear?

**To diminish your fears, you need only to develop more trust
in your ability to handle whatever comes your way.**

We cannot escape fear. We can only transform it into a companion that accompanies us in all our exciting adventures; it is not an anchor holding us transfixed in one spot. If everybody feels fear when approaching something totally new in life, yet so many are out there "doing it" despite the fear, then we must conclude that:

FEAR IS NOT THE PROBLEM.

The real issue has nothing to do with the fear itself, but, rather, *how we hold the fear*. For some, fear is totally irrelevant. They hold their fear from a position of power (choice, energy and action). For others, it creates a state of paralysis. These people hold their fear from a position of pain (helplessness, depression and paralysis).

A.   **The secret is to move yourself from a position of pain, to a position of power.**

<u>How We Hold Fear</u>

<u>PAIN</u>	<u>POWER</u>
Helplessness	CHOICE
Depression	EXCITEMENT
Paralysis	ACTION

POWER meaning power over your perceptions of the world.
POWER meaning power over how you react to situations in your life.
POWER to do what is necessary for your own self-growth.
POWER to create joy and satisfaction in your life.
POWER to act.
POWER to love.

Excerpts adapted from FEEL THE FEAR AND DO IT ANYWAY, copyright © 1987 by Susan Jeffers, reprinted by permission of Harcourt Brace & Company. Pages 29, 33-34.

B.   To Help Move From a Path of Pain to a Path of Power.....

Choose to move to a Pain-to-Power Vocabulary as follows:

Pain	POWER
I can't	I won't
I should	I could
It's not my fault	I am responsible for...
It's a problem	It's an opportunity
I'm never satisfied	I want to learn and grow
Life's a struggle	Life's an adventure
I hope	I know
If only	Next time
What will I do?	I know I can handle it
It's terrible	It's a learning experience

"I can't" implies you have no control over your life whereas **"I won't"** puts a situation in the realm of choices. When you give your power away to someone or something else, you move farther from power to pain. As a result, you decrease your ability to handle the fear in your life.

THE TRUTH IS YOU REALLY ARE IN CONTROL—IN TOTAL CONTROL

It is difficult to accept the fact that you are the cause of the feelings that take away your joy in life. It is very upsetting when you begin to see yourself as your own worst enemy. On the other hand, this realization is your biggest blessing. If you know you can create your own misery, it stands to reason that you can also create your own joy. Begin to take responsibility for your life. Responsibility = the ability to respond.

C.   Seven Definitions of Taking Responsibility

1. Taking responsibility means never blaming anyone else for anything else your being, doing, having or feeling.

2. Taking responsibility means not blaming yourself.

Excerpts adapted from FEEL THE FEAR AND DO IT ANYWAY, copyright © 1987 by Susan Jeffers, reprinted by permission of Harcourt Brace & Company. Pages 39-40, 51-52, 54.

3. Taking responsibility means being aware of where and when you are NOT taking responsibility so that you can eventually change.

4. Taking responsibility means handling the chatterbox. This is the little voice inside that tries to drive you crazy—and often succeeds! It's the voice that heralds doom, lack and losing. We're so used to its presence we often don't even notice it is talking to us. It holds the key to all you r fears.

5. Taking responsibility means being aware of payoffs that keep you "stuck." Example: Speaking to others about the grief men have caused in our lives by always doing something to take away our happiness. The payoff was that we didn't have to create our own happiness—we could simply blame men for not giving it to us.

6. Taking responsibility means figuring out what you want in life and acting on it. Set your goals—and work toward them. Most of us do not "sculpt" our lives. We accept what comes our way.

7. Taking responsibility means being aware of the multitude of choices you have in any given situation.

THE KNOWLEDGE THAT YOU CAN HANDLE ANYTHING THAT COMES YOUR WAY IS THE KEY TO ALLOWING YOURSELF TO TAKE RISKS. SECURITY IS NOT HAVING THINGS; IT'S HANDLING THINGS.

D. **Seven Ways to Reclaim Your Power**

1. Avoid casting blame on an external force for your bad feelings about life. Nothing outside yourself can control your thinking or your actions.

2. Avoid blaming yourself for not being in control. You are doing the best you can and you are on the way to reclaiming your power.

3. Be aware of when and where you are playing the victim role. Learn the clues that tell you that you are not being responsible for what you are being, having, doing or feeling.

4. Familiarize yourself with your biggest enemy—Your Chatterbox. Replace it with a loving internal friend.

5. Figure out the payoffs that keep you "stuck." Paradoxically, once you find them, you will probably be able to become "unstuck."

6. Determine what you want in life and act on it. Stop waiting for someone to give it to you. You'll be waiting a long time.

7. Be aware of the many choices you have—in both actions and feelings—in any situation that comes your way. Choose the path that contributes to your growth and makes you feel at peace with yourself and others.

STOP FEEDING YOURSELF NEGATIVE THOUGHTS. NEGATIVE THOUGHTS TAKE AWAY YOUR POWER. OUTTALK YOUR NEGATIVITY!

When I tune into my **CHATTERBOX**	When I tune into my **HIGHER SELF**
I try to control	**I trust**
I don't notice my blessings	**I appreciate**
I need	**I love**
I am insensitive	**I care**
I am in turmoil	**I am at peace**
I am blocked	**I am creative**
I don't know I count	**I count**
I repel	**I attract**
I am bored	**I am involved**
I am filled with self-doubt	**I am confident**
I am dissatisfied	**I am content**
I wait and wait	**I live now**
I hold resentment	**I forgive**
I am tense	**I am relaxed**
I am a robot	**I am alive**
I am being passed by	**I love getting older**
I am weak	**I am powerful**
I am vulnerable	**I am protected**
I am lonely	**I am connected**
I am afraid	**I am excited**

Excerpts adapted from FEEL THE FEAR AND DO IT ANYWAY, copyright © 1987 by Susan Jeffers, reprinted by permission of Harcourt Brace & Company. Pages 67-68, 76, 79-80.

MAKING DECISIONS

One of the biggest fears that keeps us from moving ahead in our lives is our difficulty in making decisions. The irony, of course, is that by not choosing, we **are** choosing. We have been taught "Be careful! You might make the wrong decision!" We fear the wrong decision will deprive us of something—money, friends, lovers, status or whatever the right decision is supposed to bring us.

Every time you encounter something that forces you to "handle it," your self-esteem is raised considerably. You learn to trust that you will survive, no matter what happens. And in this way your fears are diminished immeasurably.

A. BEFORE MAKING A DECISION

1. **Focus immediately on the No-Lose Model.** Affirm to yourself, "I can't lose—regardless of the outcome of the decision I make." Look forward to the opportunities for learning and growing that either pathway gives you. Push out thoughts of what you can lose and allow only thoughts of what can be gained.

2. **Do your homework.** There is much to learn about the alternatives that lie before you. Don't be afraid to approach professionals relative to the decision to be made. Look for feedback from other sources as well.

3. **Establish your priorities.** This will require some soul-searching. Give yourself time to really think about what you want out of life. This is a very difficult thing to discover for most of us, since we were trained at an early age to do what other people want us to do. We are out of touch with those things that really bring us satisfaction. Allow yourself confusion in the searching process. It is through confusion that you finally come to clarity.

4. **Trust your impulses.** Your body gives some good clues about which way to go. Don't be afraid to trust it.

5. **Lighten up!** We tend to take ourselves too seriously. Each experience we encounter is a valuable lesson to be learned. Whatever happens as a result of your decision, you'll handle it!

Excerpts adapted from FEEL THE FEAR AND DO IT ANYWAY, copyright © 1987 by Susan Jeffers, reprinted by permission of Harcourt Brace & Company. Pages 111, 117, 119, 121-123.

FINDING A BALANCE

Purpose of Session:

1. Identify all the parts of our lives we are striving to balance, and explore what keeps members grounded
2. Explore the process versus the content of our lives
3. Allow members to experience being grounded/balanced

Time	Activity	Purpose
5 minutes	Centering Activity: "Five Breath Vacation" by Martha Belknap.	Become focused and present centered.
15 minutes	Circle of Personal Power	Allow members to share immediate thoughts and feelings.
5 minutes	Exercise: On a board or large pad, ask members for input on what they are currently balancing in their lives.	Raise awareness of the many responsibilities and needs of members. Personalize the activity.
10 minutes	Activity: Balloon Toss (Facilitation guide on the following page)	Experiential activity using balloons as a metaphor to how we juggle different aspects of our lives: the priorities we set, the speed and accuracy with which we approach a problem, and if we are learning from our experiences.

15 minutes	How are the objects we used similar to our responsibilities? What is happening in your life when you drop the "balloon"? What distracts you from your life? What are the exceptions to your distractions? How can you experience more exceptions? What are you doing well that enables you to maintain a balance in life?	Allow members to explore metaphorically how they are balancing their lives and how they become distracted. Share they become insights into how to stay grounded and areas to set goals in for the future. Explore coping mechanisms that assist in balancing these items.
20 minutes	Read information sheets on "Trying to Find a Balance" together. Discuss the tenets of resistance and power.	Enlighten members with examples and humor on how participating in the rat race can add to our feelings of frustration and craziness.
10 minutes	Activity: Yurt Circle (Guide to facilitation on following page)	End session with members feeling a sense of support and leaving with a metaphor for being grounded and supported.
10 minutes	Closure: Journal around what members will take from this session. What coping skills do I want to maintain and strengthen? What are two things I learned or became aware of during this session?	Allow members to write about their experience and to identify concrete skills that are contributing to their success in balancing their lives.

MATERIALS NEEDED:

Board and chalk (or pad and markers)
Balloons
Journals/Pens

DIRECTIONS FOR BALLOON TOSS:

Blow up several balloons (more participants than balloons). After identifying the people, possessions, responsibilities, and goals members are striving to balance, initiate the balloon toss. Have members stand in an area clear of chairs or other obstacles they could potentially be hurt on. Encourage fun and lightheartedness. Ask members to simply keep the balloons off the ground as best they can. Whenever a balloon comes to you, simply hit it up in the air. After several minutes, prepare members with these instructions: when you give the word "STOP," they are instructed to catch a balloon. It must be caught in mid-air and not taken off the ground. Once members catch them, repeat the activity.

Processing can focus around tools members use and inevitably some things still fall through the cracks. Identify that when we are doing the best that we can, blaming ourselves for not finishing a task, or not performing to our level of expectations, is not worth the negative energy it creates inside of us. Address the difference between hope and expectations. There are no alternatives in expectations. If we do not get it, we are disappointed. When we hope, we leave the universe open and are less likely to be disappointed.

Photo by Tim Athey

Photo by Tim Athey

DIRECTIONS FOR THE YURT CIRCLE:

Gather members into a circle, standing, and ask if anyone is familiar yurts—where they came from and how they are constructed. A yurt is a Mongolian structure that is unique in its design. Instead of using nails, a yurt is constructed with balance. What keeps the structure standing is how the boards lean against each other in equal pull. The group is going to construct a "yurt circle." Ask members to join hands, take a couple of steps backwards, and put their feet together. Count off by 1's and 2's. On a signal from you, 1's will lean in and 2's will lean out. Ask members to picture themselves bending from the ankles, as opposed to the knees or hips, and only leaning as far as their partners are able to hold them, or they may fall to the ground. Propose safety concerns and anyone with bad shoulders, arms, or ankles may want to rest this one out. After their first try, ask what may help them out when they do it again. This time 2's lean in. Other variations may include switching without stopping as in a consecutive turn of 1's in and then 1's out.

FIVE BREATH VACATION

Purpose: quiet relaxation between activities

Sit comfortably and close your eyes.

Be aware of your breathing.

Listen to the sound of your breath.

Feel the air flowing gently in and out.

On your next breath, imagine a beautiful place you'd like to visit.

As you breathe out, feel yourself traveling there.

On your second breath in, notice the colors of your favorite place.

As you breathe out, enjoy this scene in every possible way.

On your third breath in, listen to the natural sounds of this place.

As you breathe out, be aware of the quietness you feel inside yourself.

On your fourth breath in, notice all the beauty surrounding you.

As you breath out, relax into full enjoyment of this time and place.

On your fifth breath in, feel yourself traveling home again.

As you breathe out, stretch your arms and open your eyes.

Tell someone about your wonderful five breath vacation.

From *Taming Your Dragons* by M. Belknap. Page 22.
Reprinted by permission of Martha Belknap, 1170 Dixon Road/Gold Hill, Boulder, CO 80302.

TRYING TO FIND A BALANCE

We spend our lives trying to alter externals, trying to get what we want, trying to manipulate the "whats." Relationships, friends, lovers, money, possessions, values, opinions, ideas, life, hopes, dreams, children, jobs, death, education, etc., are "whats."

Whats come and go.   Whats pass.

Peace, joy and freedom lie in real-izing the how, the process, rather than the content of life. We get so caught up in the specifics, the "whats" of life, that we can't step back and see the broader view, the whole, the process, how it is. We don't realize that we experience our lives the way we do, not because they actually are that way, but because that's how we see them.

It's not what you do, it's how you do it.
It's not what you see, it's how you see it.
It's not what you think, it's how you think it.
It's not what you feel, it's how you feel it.

Consider these definitions:

wrong \rong\ n.	Not the way I want it.
right \rite\ adj.	The way I think it should be.
good \gud\ adj.	Whatever I like (at the moment).
bad \bad\ adj.	Whatever I don't like (at the moment).

What are your definitions of the following words, not as defined by Webster or society, but as you honestly experience them?

wrong	bad	want	equal
right	honest	security	
fair	selfish	enough	
good	need	loving	

It is important to realize that these are your definitions and not everyone's........

HOW DO YOU FEEL WHEN YOU...	HOW DO YOU KEEP YOURSELF FROM...
slow down	slowing down
relax	relaxing
stop	stopping

From The Key and the Name of the Key is Willingness. Pages 2-5, 10.
Copyright 1984 by A Center for the Practice of Zen Buddhist Meditation. Reprinted by permission.

Being the fastest, the richest, the thinnest, the smartest on the treadmill won't prove anything. There's nothing to prove, nothing to win, nothing to get.

NO ONE, NO THING, CAN TAKE YOUR PEACE, YOUR JOY, YOUR ADEQUACY, AWAY FROM YOU. YOU HAVE TO GIVE IT UP VOLUNTARILY.

And we give it up so easily, for just about anything: other people's opinions, late meals, long lines, red lights.... The odds of anyone ever getting all or even most of what she/he wants, at any given time are very slim. There are always irresponsible, late, rude, inept, stupid people;

A lack of
     parking places, appointments available, money, promotions, weekends, dates, affection, sex;

An excess of
     criticism, judgements, things spilled on clothes, unexpected guests, red lights...

**YOU HAVE NO CHOICE ABOUT WHAT YOU GET.
YOU HAVE ABSOLUTE CHOICE ABOUT WHAT YOU DO.**

Could be, should be, ought to be, might be, hope will be, wish could be, want to be, are postures we maintain to avoid accepting what **is**,   to remain ignore-ant of what **is**.

In this way we manage to avoid the only time in which we live. Our lives consist of "what **is**" in the present moment.

WHEN YOU STOP COMPARING WHAT IS RIGHT HERE AND NOW
WITH WHAT YOU WISH WERE, YOU CAN BEGIN TO ENJOY WHAT IS.

Until we learn to accept, we cling to things being the way they have been, or we wish they were, or want them to be, or hope they will be. We tense up all our muscles, dig in our heels, and **RESIST**. Then we believe that the energy we have put into resisting change is actually maintaining the status quo. We actually begin to believe that we are holding things together. Then we draw the conclusion: I am in control. And that conclusion is an illusion.
**When we learn to accept everything that comes into our lives,
we are free from the pain of resistance.**

Resistance does not work.

Choice #1:   You can accept what is.   Choice #2:   You can resist what is.

In acceptance there is peace. In resistance there is pain. The choice is always ours.

WHAT ARE YOU RESISTING IN YOUR LIFE?

YOU, each moment, contain all that is, everything you seek. When you know that, when you "come from" that, you see perfection and complete adequacy all around you. When you don't know that, when you don't "come from" that, you spend all your time trying to manipulate externals so that you get whatever you think you need to make you feel "enough." (That's known as adding legs to a painted snake or putting another head on the one you already have.)

THE WAYS YOU THINK YOU ARE, NOT THE WAYS YOU REALLY ARE, ARE THE BARS ON YOUR OWN PERSONAL PRISON.

Please recall: Just because you think something is so (that you're bad, selfish, ugly, perfect, brilliant, superior, inadequate) doesn't mean it is so.
<u>It only means that you think it's so.</u>

You are doing your life. Not that you are responsible in the sense that you are to blame or that you have caused it—just that your reactions, responses, feelings, thoughts, ideas, attitudes, theories, standards, beliefs, likes, dislikes, wants, needs, etc. are yours. They create your world. And it is **THIS** which you must face honestly and learn to love and accept through compassion.

We do what we do for the joy of doing, not because we're going to get a reward when it's over (or the odds are real good that we'll be disappointed a lot). You know what's right for you each moment. Not fun or pleasurable or exciting—just right. Deep down in your bones, in your insides, in your heart, it may take some practice before you trust that you have that knowingness about everything, and if you pay attention, that knowingness is already guiding you through your life.
TO THE DEGREE THAT YOU KNOW IT, DO IT.

Not because you "should," or you'd "better," just because it feels good to do what you know is right!

THAT WHICH IS UNACCEPTABLE TO YOU EXISTS ONLY THROUGH THE POWER WHICH YOU GIVE IT.

From *The Key and the Name of the Key is Willingness.* Pages 33-35, 38-40, 56, 74.
Copyright 1984 by A Center for the Practice of Zen Buddhist Meditation. Reprinted by permission.

We want the externals to be the cause of who we are; in fact, the externals are the result of who we are. Seeing oneself as a victim is a choice, not a requirement. At any time, one can choose to be......

Your world continues to be the same, not because that's the way the world is, but because you continue to make the same choices. If you really want to do it differently, you're going to have to find the **willingness** to stop punishing, criticizing, judging, beating and otherwise "improving" yourself. We always do what is truly our first priority. Don't be confused by what you say is most important to you.

WATCH WHAT YOU DO.

What you do is what is most important to you. If the answers were in the places you've been looking...   externals...   objective reality...

you would have already have found them. Obviously, if the way you've been doing it worked, you wouldn't still be looking for answers. And yet our fear...

> of doing it differently,
> of facing the unknown,
> of going against society,
> of questioning our conditioning,

...is so great, that we continue to follow the same patterns over and over, even when we know full-well that they lead to unhappiness.

WE CONTINUE TO CHOOSE OUR BELIEFS OVER OUR EXPERIENCE.

We feel vulnerable because we don't trust that the love, wisdom and compassion we need will be there when we need it.

We have identified with a small, separate self who suffers and we have forgotten that that's not who we really are. That which you are seeking is causing you to seek. As long as you're looking outward, you're looking in the wrong direction.

YOUR LIFE CAN BE DIFFERENT IN ANY MOMENT YOU
CHOOSE TO CHANGE YOUR CHOICES.
WHEN WE'RE TOO BUSY TO PAY ATTENTION,
WE'RE CHOOSING IGNORANCE.

PAIN AND SUFFERING

Purpose of Session:

1. Self-exploration of the relationship between our choices and pain and suffering
2. Use of a story as a metaphor depicting pain and suffering, offering a solution to that pain
3. Sharing tools that allow for peace of mind and healthy choices

Time	Activity	Purpose
5 minutes	Centering Activity: "Music in the Trees" by Martha Belknap.	Assist members in becoming centered and present focused.
15 minutes	Circle of Personal Power	Allow members to share immediate thoughts and feelings.
10 minutes	Read "The Bridge" by Edwin Friedman. Laying a rope in the middle of the group during the story is effective for visual learners. Asking members to hold a part of the rope while the story is being read is effective for kinesthetic learners.	Metaphor bringing choices and our responsibility for our reactions and emotions into the light.
40 minutes	Process: What was it like holding the rope? Are you currently holding a rope in your life? Why is it so difficult to let go once we are experiencing "rope burn"? Why are the dependent so often calling the shots? How much responsibility does the man on the bridge have for the other? Could both men be the same person? How are	Draw from the experiences of members and what came up for them during the story. Reflect upon the story's metaphor of holding a rope, other people feeling

	acceptance, gratitude, and detachment part of the solution?	stuck and powerless, and freeing ourselves through our respect for choices.
25 minutes	Read "Pain and Suffering" information sheets to pull out more tools to be used in our responses to situations in our lives.	Focus on solutions and how choices, acceptance, and detachment are ways to free ourselves from unnecessary pain and suffering.
5 minutes	Closure: Journal: What will you take from today's group? What has been significant and/or fits with something you are currently experiencing?	Allow members to process what was experienced in group and set goals related to the tools.

MATERIALS NEEDED:

    Journals

    Pens

    Rope

MUSIC IN THE TREES

Purpose: develop sense of hearing

Relax in whatever way you are the most comfortable.
Close your eyes and pretend that you are camping in the forest.
The sun is just beginning to come up.

The air is getting warmer.
Listen to the sounds around you.   (long pause)
A bee is buzzing in the dandelions.

A cricket is chirping in the grass.
A chipmunk is scurrying across a log.
A squirrel is chewing on an acorn.

Some bluejays are chattering in the bushes.
What other sounds can you hear?   (long pause)
Some fairies are hiding under the mushrooms.

They are playing their violins.
Some elves are sitting on top of the buttercups.
They are playing their magical harps.

Some leprechauns are perched on the root of a tree trunk.
They all have tiny flutes.
A goblin is tapping on a tree stump.   Listen to the orchestra!

What other instruments can you hear?
Pretend that you are the conductor of this woodland symphony.
Listen to the music in the trees!

From *Taming Your Dragons* by M. Belknap. Page 37. Reprinted by permission of
Martha Belknap, 1170 Dixon Road/Gold Hill, Boulder, CO 80302.

THE BRIDGE

There was a man who had given much thought to what he wanted from life. He had experienced many moods and trials. He had experimented with different ways of living, and he had had his share of both success and failure. At last, he began to see clearly where he wanted to go.

Diligently, he searched for the right opportunity. Sometimes he came close, only to be pushed away. Often he applied all his strength and imagination, only to find the path hopelessly blocked. And then at last it came. But the opportunity would not wait. It would be made available only for a short time. If it were seen that he was not committed, the opportunity would not come again.

Eager to arrive, he started on his journey. With each step, he wanted to move faster; with each thought about his goal, his heart beat quicker; with each vision of what lay ahead, he found renewed vigor. Strength that had left him since his early youth returned, and desires, all kinds of desires, reawakened from their long-dormant positions.

Hurrying along, he came upon a bridge that crossed through the middle of a town. It has been built high above a river in order to protect it from the floods of spring.

He started across. Then he noticed someone coming from the opposite direction. As they moved closer, it seemed as though the other were coming to greet him. He could see clearly, however, that he did not know this other, who was dressed similarly except for something tied around his waist.

When they were within hailing distance, he could see that what the other had about his waist was a rope. It was wrapped around him many times and probably, if extended, would reach a length of 30 feet.

The other began to uncurl the rope, and just as they were coming close, the stranger said, "Pardon me, would you be so kind as to hold the end a moment?"
Surprised by this politely phrased but curious request, he agreed without a thought, reached out, and took it.

"Thank you," said the other, who then added, "two hands now, and remember, hold tight."
Whereupon, the other jumped off the bridge.

Quickly, the free-falling body hurtled the distance of the rope's length, and from the bridge the man abruptly felt the pull. Instinctively, he held tight and was almost dragged over the side. He managed to brace himself against the edge, however, and after having caught his breath, looked down at the other dangling, close to oblivion.

"What are you trying to do?" he yelled.

"Just hold tight," said the other.

"This is ridiculous," the man thought and began trying to haul the other in. He could not get the leverage, however. It was as though the weight of the other person and the length of the rope had been carefully calculated in advance so that together they created a counterweight just beyond his strength to bring the other back to safety. "Why did you do this?" the man called out.

"Remember," said the other, "if you let go, I will be lost."

"But I cannot pull you up," the man cried.

"I am your responsibility," said the other.

"Well, I did not ask for it," the man said.

"If you let go, I am lost," repeated the other.

He began to look around for help. But there was no one. How long would he have to wait? Why did this happen to befall him now, just as he was on the verge of true success? He examined the side, searching for a place to tie the rope. Some protrusion, perhaps, or maybe a hole in the boards. But the railing was unusually uniform in shape; there were no spaces between the boards. There was no way to get rid of this newfound burden even temporarily.

"What do you want?" he asked the other hanging below.

"Just your help," the other answered.
"How can I help? I cannot pull you in, and there is no place to tie the rope so that I can go and find someone to help me help you."

"I know that. Just hang on; that will be enough. Tie the rope around your waist; it will be easier. " Fearing that his arms could not hold out much longer, he tied the rope around his waist.

"Why did you do this?" he asked again. "Don't you see what you have done? What possible purpose could you have had in mind?"

"Just remember," said the other, "my life is in your hands."
What should he do?

"If I let go, all my life I will know that I let this other die. If I stay, I risk losing my momentum toward my own long-sought-after salvation. Either way this will haunt me forever. " With ironic humor he thought to die himself, instantly, to jump off the bridge while still holding on. "That would teach this fool." But he wanted to live and to live life fully. "What a choice I have to make; how shall I ever decide?"

As time went by, still no one came. The critical moment of decision was drawing near. To show his commitment to his own goals, he would have to continue on his journey now. It was already almost too late to arrive in time. But what a terrible choice to have to make.
A new thought occurred to him. While he could not pull this other up solely by his own efforts, if the other would shorten the rope from his end by curling it around his waist again and again, together they could do it. Actually, the other could do it by himself, so long as he, standing on the bridge, kept it still and steady.

"Now listen," he shouted down. "I think I know how to save you." And he explained his plan. But the other wasn't interested.

"You mean you won't help? But I told you I cannot pull you up myself, and I don't think I can hang on much longer either."

"You must try," the other shouted back in tears. "If you fail, I die."

The point of decision arrived. What should he do? "My life or this other's?" And then a new idea. A revelation. So new, in fact, it seemed heretical, so alien was it to his traditional way of thinking.

"I want you to listen carefully," he said, "because I mean what I am about to say. I will not accept the position of choice for your life, only for my own; the position of choice for your own life I hereby give back to you."

"What do you mean?" the other asked, afraid.

"I mean, simply, it's up to you. You decide which way this ends. I will become the counterweight. You do the pulling and bring yourself up. I will even tug a little from here. "

He began unwinding the rope from around his waist and braced himself anew against the side.

"You cannot mean what you say," the other shrieked. "You would not be so selfish. I am your responsibility. What could be so important that you would let someone die? Do not do this to me."

He waited a moment. There was no change in the tension of the rope.

"I accept your choice," he said, at last, and freed his hands.

From *Friedman's Fables* by E. H. Friedman. Pages 9-13. Published by The Guilford Press.
Reprinted by permission.

PAIN AND SUFFERING

Pain is not suffering. Suffering is our reaction to pain. Defensiveness, greed, anger, denial, repression, rejection, hatred, fear—to name a few—are all, at their source, reactions to pain. Pain is a "something" to be gotten rid of, or prevented. "I don't want this pain," "get rid of this," "something's wrong with me," "this shouldn't be happening" are all things we might say during a painful experience. We take pain and add suffering to it until the two are so intertwined that it's easy to see why we take the two words to mean the same thing.

The suffering we add to pain is often after the fact. I have a painful experience, then I try to figure out how I can arrange my life so that I don't experience that pain again. I am willing to make sacrifices for security, for control. For instance, I might stay with work I hate because I'm afraid of not being able to find something else, or afraid of being dependent —both painful experiences. Or having experienced the pain of an unrequited love, I now say good-bye to lovers before they can say good-bye to me.

WE SUFFER WHEN WE ARE NOT WILLING TO FEEL PAIN.

We close ourselves off. We dig trenches. We put up barricades. We develop "sensitive" radar systems. And when provoked, we attack. All because we don't want to feel pain. We are vulnerable in its presence—vulnerable to being found out. Because when we stay with pain and don't add suffering to it by closing ourselves off, we see that we are in fact equal to that pain, that we can "take it."

We see through the game of inadequacy.

We see the wholeness and truth of our essential being. And we see that, like everything else, no one pain lasts forever.

I HAVE LOST MY FAVORITE TEACUP.
I HAVE TWO CHOICES.

I can have lost my
teacup and be
miserable.

I can have lost my
teacup and be
all right.

From *That Which You Are Seeking is Causing You To Seek.* Pages 17-20.
Copyright 1990 by A Center for Zen Buddhist Meditation. Reprinted by permission.

In either case, the teacup is gone.

THE DEGREE TO WHICH I AM PROUD/DELIGHTED/SMUG WHEN I AM "RIGHT" IS THE DEGREE TO WHICH I WILL SUFFER WHEN I AM "WRONG." IF I DON'T NEED TO TAKE CREDIT, I DON'T NEED TO TAKE BLAME.

"Letting go" does not mean "not having." We let go of our **attachment to getting** what we want. We aren't required to let go of the "what," the object of our desire. And if we let go of that attachment, the odds of getting what we want will be just as good as ever. The only real difference will be that we won't suffer if we don't get it.

What if you could be as happy as you can be and not be getting what you want?

Letting go is releasing our grip on delusion, allowing us to see what is. When we stop resisting what is, when we stop clinging to our beliefs and assumptions about how things should be, we are letting go, we are opening ourselves to the present moment.

LETTING GO GOES HAND IN HAND WITH ACCEPTANCE. ONE DOES NOT OCCUR WITHOUT THE OTHER. LETTING GO IS OPENING THE HAND. ACCEPTANCE IS WHAT THE OPEN HAND RECEIVES.

Joy is not the product of getting what you want (more money, long vacations, perfect health, new lover, total security, thinner thighs, better job...).

JOY is compassion turned inward— the end of struggle, the end of competition.

"What makes us do something we know will make us miserable? It seems that we choose to suffer." We see ourselves going down the same roads over and over again. We begin to see that they lead to suffering, and yet we continue to choose them almost as if we didn't know how to do anything else. I overeat, I feel sick and hate myself. I fall in love, the object of my affection rejects or betrays me. I feel depressed, I go on a buying binge and regret it later. The suffering is in my response to what is.

IF YOU WANT TO END YOUR SUFFERING, STOP IDENTIFYING WITH THE PROCESS THAT'S CAUSING IT.

I begin to suspect a pay-off. Would I find myself in the same fix over and over again if I didn't get something out of it? Probably not. So what is this payoff? The pay-off is in knowing who I am as a familiar, separate self. I am unlovable, I am self-indulgent. But most important of all, I am separate...and I experience separateness when I resist what is.

WHEN WE UNDERSTAND HOW WE DO SOMETHING, WE ARE FREE TO CHANGE IT.

We stop identifying with the process that maintains our suffering when we stop judging ourselves, when we stop holding a club over our heads to make sure we do things right. The moment we drop all of that, we have dropped the only thing that can cause us to suffer. Profound change—change in how we do, not what we do—**happens only with complete acceptance.** Acceptance we're pointing to here has nothing to do with liking and disliking, caring or not caring. We all have a natural capacity for helping, for responding lovingly and compassionately. When we step back from the voices that are always telling us how things should be and how we should react—we provide an opportunity to experience this inherent goodness, and in our acceptance of all that is, we learn to trust our natural inclination to follow the path that leads away from suffering. We learn to respond lovingly and appropriately. We become responsible in the truest sense of the word.

It is inaccurate to equate   pain and suffering
loss and suffering
hunger and suffering
sickness and suffering
poverty and suffering

It is also inaccurate to equate   wealth and happiness
good fortune and happiness
abundance and happiness
health and happiness
beauty and happiness

Whether life is seen as a struggle or a gift depends on one's attitude of mind, not on one's circumstances.

PERCEPTIONS OF SELF

Purpose of Session:
1. Continue to build trust and cohesion among members
2. Self-exploration; real self vs. image of self
3. Increase comfort level of sharing

Time	Activity	Purpose
5 minutes	Centering Activity: "Become Your Favorite Cat" by Martha Belknap.	Focus group to become present centered.
15 minutes	Circle of Personal Power	Allow members to share immediate thoughts/feelings.
10 minutes	Introduction to topic of how we perceive ourselves. Relate this back to the centering activity and if members felt self-conscious and why. Give each member a piece of clay (or playdough) and ask them to mold the clay to represent a metaphor of the perception they have of themselves. "How do you see yourself?" Listening to instrumental music is also helpful in setting the tone for introspection.	Transfer self-perception to a tactile activity to further increase insights and self-awareness.
15 minutes	Sharing their figures.	Allow members to share what their figure represents. Try to hold comments until the end of the session.

5 minutes	With a new piece of clay (or playdough), ask members to mold a figure depicting how they feel others perceive them.	While transferring perception to a tactile figure, members gain an awareness of the real self vs. an image.
15 minutes	Sharing their figures.	Continue to ask members to hold their comments. Sharing without defending is the goal.
20 minutes	Option (1): If the group has been together for some time, ask if there are members who would be willing to hear how other members actually perceive them. Feedback from members can be powerful and help alleviate untrue perceptions. Use your judgment.	Allow members a chance to gain such feedback in a safe and supportive environment.
	Option (2): Ask members to alter one of their two figures, remolding the figure into how they would like others to view them, or how they would like to see themselves differently in some way.	To allow members an opportunity to make changes tactilely, and to have a visual representation of the results of those changes.
5 minutes	Closing. Journal members' thoughts from this session and identify feelings and how this session may be useful to them in the future.	Allow members to reflect upon what was said, heard, and felt today.

MATERIALS NEEDED:

        Clay or playdough
        Paper towels
        Music player and tape
        Journals
        Pens

Photo by Tim Athey

BECOME YOUR FAVORITE CAT

Purpose: stretch your chest and middle back

Kneel down on all fours like a cat.

Breathe in slowly through your nose.

As you breathe out, bring your right knee toward your nose,

Feel the curl in your back as you hold the stretch.

Breathe in and lift your right leg in the air behind you.

Lift your head and look up.

Feel the arch in your back as you hold the stretch.

Breathe out and return to all fours.

Rest and notice how you feel.

Repeat the stretch with your left leg.

Breathe out and return to all fours.

Now me-ow like your favorite cat!

From *Taming Your Dragons* by M. Belknap. Page 15. Reprinted by permission of
Martha Belknap, 1170 Dixon Road/Gold Hill, Boulder, CO 80302.

PROJECTION

It is good to recognize that the expectations of others, the standards they expect us to meet, are really our own projections. We judge ourselves by our standards, project them onto other people, then believe they think those things about us.

A POSSIBLE SCENARIO
I'm depressed; I hate being depressed; I'm judging myself for being depressed.
I look at my friends; I think they hate it when I'm depressed; I think they are judging me.

IN FACT
They may have no reaction to it at all. They may not even notice.
It's **my** standards that aren't met.

YES, BUT
What if they tell me they hate my depression?

If your friends tell you they hate your depression, you can know that that's their problem just as it would be your problem if you hated theirs. We tend to dislike and avoid in others what we're not willing to face in ourselves. If I see a problem, it's mine. My eyes saw it; it appeared in my head; it came out of my mouth.

The ways I think the world expects me to be are the ways I've been taught to believe I should be. People are judging and criticizing and dismissing me all the time, but as long as I'm meeting my standards of how I should be, I don't even notice. As soon as I don't meet my standards, I think other people are judging me as harshly as I'm judging myself.

ARE YOU WILLING TO GIVE UP YOUR LIFE FOR WHAT YOU THINK OTHER PEOPLE MIGHT BE THINKING?

HAS GIVING UP YOUR OWN LIFE BROUGHT THE ACCEPTANCE AND APPROVAL THAT YOU'VE ALWAYS WANTED?

HAS NOT BEING WHO YOU REALLY ARE BROUGHT THE JOY AND FULFILLMENT YOU'VE BEEN SEEKING?

From *The Depression Book. Depression as an Opportunity for Growth.* Pages 98-100.
Copyright 1991 by A Center for Zen Buddhist Meditation. Reprinted by permission.

We deny ourselves our life, close our options because we think society expects us to, we think people will judge us, we think it's too selfish to do otherwise. We take the path that seems safest. Then, because we're depressing our passion, our desire for life, we eventually move into despair and ask ourselves, why go on?   A valid question.

We end up with just the hard stuff, the shoulds, the have to's, the things we're trying to avoid in the first place. We wind up with emptiness---exhaustion-----meaninglessness.
The good news is none of what society or culture tried to get you to believe was true in the first place. There never have been any limits. There never was anything wrong with you...   and there still isn't.

You can be whatever you choose, and the proof of that is that you are now.

If what we think is wrong with us were really wrong with us, we would have been able to fix it by now.... The fact that we haven't been able to fix it is the proof that it's not really the problem. The problem is that we have been taught to believe there's a problem. It's like being told that something is broken and trying and trying to fix it and never succeeding...
                                                                    because it isn't broken.

THERE IS NO PROBLEM. STOP CREATING ONE.
FEELING GUILTY OVER BEING WHO YOU ARE DOES
NOTHING BUT ROB YOU OF YOUR LIFE.

CAN YOU BE OPEN TO THE POSSIBILITY THAT IF YOU WERE WHO YOU REALLY ARE, YOU
WOULD HAVE THE APPROVAL AND ACCEPTANCE YOU'VE ALWAYS WANTED?
FROM YOURSELF IF FROM NO ONE ELSE?

When it comes right down to it, it doesn't really matter to us what others think of us. They criticize us and we're defensive. They compliment us and we don't believe them. The only praise we really accept is from ourselves. When _we_ feel satisfied with what we've done, we're pleased.

HERE'S HOW IT WORKS IN PART:

LOOP: I won't be who I am because I'm afraid others won't approve..... I try to be who I "should" be and I don't approve..... I don't approve of me..... I project that disapproval onto others and then believe they disapprove of me..... I feel disapproved of..... therefore, it seems that I have proof that there's something wrong with me.

And there kind of is......

I'm caught in this awful loop of my own making. Irony: We endlessly seek other people's approval when the only approval that means anything to us is our own.

IF I'M LIVING THE LIFE I WANT TO LIVE, IT'S CLEAR THAT NOBODY OWES ME ANYTHING, AND FROM THAT PLACE OF BEING SATISFIED, I CAN BE MUCH MORE GENEROUS.

WHEN YOU'VE SUFFERED ENOUGH, YOU'LL REMEMBER THAT YOU KNOW HOW TO DO IT.

THE SKIN HORSE

The Skin Horse had lived longer in the nursery than any of the others. He was so old that his brown coat was bald in patches and showed the seams underneath, and most of the hairs in his tail had been pulled out to string bead necklaces. He was wise, for he had seen a long succession of mechanical toys arrive to boast and swagger, and by-and-by break their mainsprings and pass away, and he knew that they were only toys, and would never turn into anything else. For nursery magic is very strange and wonderful, and only those playthings that are old and wise and experienced, like the Skin Horse, understand all about it.

"What is REAL?" asked the Rabbit one day, when they were lying side by side near the nursery fender, before Nana came to tidy the room. "Does it mean having things that buzz inside you and a stick-out handle?"

"Real isn't how you are made," said the Skin Horse. "It's a thing that happens to you. When a child loves you for a long, long time, not just to play with, but REALLY loves you, then you become Real."

"Sometimes," said the Skin Horse, for he was always truthful, "when you are Real you don't mind being hurt."

"Does it happen all at once, like being wound up," he asked, "or bit by bit?"

"It doesn't happen all at once," said the Skin Horse. "You become. It takes a long time. That's why it doesn't often happen to people who break easily, or have sharp edges, or who have to be carefully kept. Generally, by the time you are Real, most of your hair has been loved off, and your eyes drop out and you get loose in the joints and very shabby. But these things don't matter at all, because once you are Real you can't be ugly, except to people who don't understand."

"I suppose you are Real?" said the Rabbit. And then he wished he had not said it, for he thought the Skin Horse might be sensitive. But the Skin Horse only smiled.

"The Boy's Uncle made me Real," he said. "That was a great many years ago; but once you are Real you can't become unreal again. It lasts for always." The Rabbit sighed. He thought it would be a long time before this magic called Real happened to him. He longed to become Real, to know what it felt like; and yet the idea of growing shabby and losing his eyes and whiskers was rather sad. He wished that he could become it without these uncomfortable things happening to him.

From *The Velveteen Rabbit* by M. Williams. Pages 2-6. Copyright 1991.
Published by Unicorn Publishing House. Reprinted by permission.

RELATIONSHIPS

Purpose of Session:
1. Gain an awareness of various dynamics played out in relationships
2. Experience the feelings involved in these relationships, tools to identify them early on, and how to respond to them.
3. Identifying tools members have in maintaining a healthy relationship

Time	Activity	Purpose
5 minutes	Centering Activity: "Magic Messages" by Martha Belknap.	Focus members.
15 minutes	Circle of Personal Power	Allow members to express immediate thoughts and feelings.
45 minutes	Activity: Sculpting Types of Love Relationships. Before members break out of each position, ask how it feels to be in that position. Continue to process after each sculpture, allowing members to express feelings. Also identify that those feelings (and our intuition that this does not feel good) are indicators for action.	Experiential activity to identify several unhealthy dynamics in a relationship.
15 minutes	Activity: Whole Life Relationship Explore what a healthy relationship looks and feels like. Emphasize that a relationship with ourselves comes first—our hobbies, spiritual life, service, family, etc., or other parts of our life. Explore the difference between need and love.	Move members to what constitutes a healthy relationship.
10 minutes	Closing. Share what information or feelings are staying with you from this session.	Allow members to reflect upon their experience.

MAGIC MESSAGES

Purpose: feel good about yourself

Relax in whatever way you are most comfortable.
Close your eyes and let go of your cheeks and jaw.
Let go of your chin and tongue.
Let your eyes roll up toward the top of your head like marbles.
Listen to your breathing.   (long pause)
Repeat these messages quietly to yourself.

> My legs are heavy and warm.
> My arms are quiet and still.
> My heartbeat is steady and even.
> My breathing is slow and deep.
> My forehead is cool.
> My whole body is comfortable.
>
> I am calm and relaxed.
> I am peaceful inside.
> I feel healthy and strong.
> I can remember what I learn.
> I can take good care of myself.
> I can make friends easily.
> I am a very special person in my family.

Think of other messages which are important to you.
Repeat them quietly to yourself.
Know that these messages are true.

From *Taming Your Dragons* by M. Belknap. Page 35. Reprinted by permission of
Martha Belknap, 1170 Dixon Road/Gold Hill, Boulder, CO 80302.

TYPES OF LOVE-RELATIONSHIPS

1. THE A-FRAME DEPENDENCY RELATIONSHIP

Photo by Tim Athey

This is the dependency relationship where two people lean on each other because they have not learned to be whole, single people by themselves. The dependency upon the other person sometimes feels good, but it is somewhat confining, and when one person wants to move or change or grow, it upsets the other person, because the other person is leaning upon her/him. Try this body sculpture with another person and then try to put into words some of the feelings that you have while you are assuming this position.

2. THE SMOTHERING RELATIONSHIP

Photo by Tim Athey

The smothering relationship is quite frequently seen in high school and teenage relationships. The vocabulary for this relationship is, "I cannot live without you. I want to spend the rest of my life with you. I will devote myself completely to making you happy. It feels so good to be so close to you." I think that many love-relationships start with this kind of a smothering relationship, but they may grow and change into something else because there is not enough space to grow when you are so close to the other person at all times. The smothering relationship tends to feel good for a while, but eventually you begin to feel trapped.

3. THE PEDESTAL

The pedestal relationship is one of worshipping the other person and saying, "I love you not for what you are, but for what I think you are. I have an idealized image of you and I would like to have you live up to that image." It is very precarious being on top of the pedestal because there are so many expectations from the other person. As with all of these relationships, you can see that there are problems of communication. Here, because you are in love with the person's idealized image, you are looking up to and trying to communicate with that image, instead of with the real person. There is a great deal of emotional distancing in this relationship, and it is difficult for the two people to become close because of the pedestal upon which one of them has been placed.

4. MASTER/SLAVE

"I am the head of this family. I am the boss. I will make the decisions around here." This relationship is not necessarily male/female with the male being the boss and head of the family. There are many females who are masters in the family, and make all the decisions. I think that in most relationships one of the partners has a personality which is a little bit stronger than the other, and I don't think that this is necessarily bad, but when the relationship becomes rigid and has no flexibility, and when one person is set up to make all of the decisions, then emotional distancing and inequality take place. The relationship that is very rigid in this posture tends to take a great deal of emotional energy in attempting to maintain one person as master and the other as slave. There is often a power struggle going on that interferes with the communication and intimacy of the relationship.

5. THE BOARDING HOUSE; BACK TO BACK

These two people are linked together by their elbows with some sort of marriage contract or an agreement that they are going to love together. There is no communication in this relationship. The typical thing is for people to come home and sit down and watch TV while they are eating, and then they retire to their living habits for the remainder of the evening. It is a loveless relationship, in the sense that there is no expression of love towards each other. Again, when you try this position, notice that when one person moves forward, changes or grows and matures, the other person is linked to that growth, and this makes it a confining relationship.

6. THE MARTYR RELATIONSHIP

The martyr is the person who completely sacrifices herself/himself in trying to serve the other people in the family. This person is always doing things for other people and never takes time for self. The martyr is the one on hands and knees in the figure above. We need to see and understand that the martyr position is a very controlling position in the sense that when the person on hands and knees moves, the other person who has a foot on the martyr is thrown off balance.

What emotion does the martyr use for gaining control? She/he controls through guilt. How can you be angry at the person who is doing everything for you, who is taking care of you completely? The martyr is very efficient at controlling people around her/him. And it is very difficult to love with a martyr because you feel so guilty that you are unable to express your own needs and to express your angry feelings. Many of you will have had a martyr parent, and it will help you to understand ways of dealing with that parent by understanding the martyr relationship.

7. THE HEALTHY LOVE RELATIONSHIP

These are two people who are whole and complete and have internal happiness within themselves. They are two upright people who are not leaning or tangled up with the other person. They are able to live their own lives. They have an abundance of life to share with the other person. So these two people choose to stay together because they are free to be two people living their lives and sharing their lives together. They can come close together and be like the smothering position; they can walk hand in hand as they might do in parenting their children; they can move apart and have their own careers and their own lives and their own friends. But they choose to stay together because of their love for each other rather than having or needing to stay together because of some unmet emotional needs. The healthy love-relationship is a relationship that gives both people the space to grow and become themselves.

From *When Your Relationship Ends*, by B. Fisher. Pages 47-49.
Copyright 1978 by Family Relations Learning Center, Inc., Boulder, CO 80521. Reprinted by permission.

WHOLE LIFE WITH RELATIONSHIP

RELATIONSHIP		

WHOLE LIFE WITHOUT RELATIONSHIP

WHOLE LIFE WITH RELATIONSHIP

CONTRIBUTION	HOBBY	LEISURE
FAMILY	ALONE TIME	PERSONAL GROWTH
WORK	RELATIONSHIP	FRIENDS

WHOLE LIFE WITHOUT RELATIONSHIP

CONTRIBUTION	HOBBY	LEISURE
FAMILY	ALONE TIME	PERSONAL GROWTH
WORK		FRIENDS

INTIMACY

We can let ourselves be close to people.

Many of us have deeply ingrained patterns for sabotaging relationships. Some of us may instinctively terminate a relationship once it moves to a certain level of closeness and intimacy.

When we start to feel close to someone, we may zero in on one of the person's character defects, then make it so big it's all we can see. We may withdraw, or push the person away to create distance. We may start criticizing the other person, a behavior sure to create distance.

We may start trying to control the person, a behavior that prevents intimacy.

We may tell ourselves we don't want or need another person, or smother the person with our needs.

Sometimes, we defeat ourselves by trying to be close to people who aren't available for intimacy—people with active addictions, or people who don't choose to be close to us. Sometimes, we choose people with particular faults so that when it comes time to be close, we have an escape hatch.

We're afraid, and we fear losing ourselves. We're afraid that closeness means we won't be able to own our power to take care of ourselves.

In recovery, we're learning that it's okay to let ourselves be close to people. We're choosing to relate to safe, healthy people, so closeness is a possibility. Closeness doesn't mean we have to lose ourselves, or our life. As one man said, we're learning that we can own our power with people, even when we're close, even when the other person has something we need.

Today, I will be available for closeness and intimacy with people, when that's appropriate. Whenever possible, I will let myself be who I am, let others be who they are, and enjoy the bond and good feelings between us.

EXPLORING THE WEDGES OF INTIMACY

What do you say, how do you act, in order to get close to others?

What do you say, how do you act, in order to keep others away?

What are the "wedges" you most often use to avoid intimacy?

When do you use them?

Are there times when you don't use them? When?

What does intimacy bring to your life?

SELF-LOVE

Purpose of Session:
1. Explore forms of self-hate and where it comes from
2. Focus on solutions and tools around self-love
3. Design and share beaded necklaces reminding us to harbor this love

Time	Activity	Purpose
5 minutes	Centering Activity: "Butterfly Wings" by Martha Belknap.	Assist members in becoming present centered.
15 minutes	Circle of Personal Power	Allow members to share immediate thoughts and feelings.
30 minutes	Discuss "Forms Self-Hate Takes" and reword them to create the "Forms of Self-Love." Explore tools to maintain self-love and enter these on board (or pad or journal).	Engage members in a a discussion revealing the ways we can sabotage our own love. Focus on the solutions to self-love.
15 minutes	Activity: Beaded Necklaces. As members design a necklace, ask them to keep in mind what each bead represents for them and how the pieces of the necklace were formed to create their necklace.	Create a visual and tactile metaphor representative of their self-love to serve as a reminder of the compassion toward self.

| 20 minutes | Process. Ask members to share their necklaces and its components. | Reinforce the love of self and share thoughts and experiences with others. |
| 10 minutes | Closing. Read "Appreciating Ourselves" by Melody Beattie. | Serves as an affirmation of the love and compassion for self. |

MATERIALS NEEDED:

Board or Pad (Chalk or Markers)
Journals/Pens
Assortment of beads
Leather or other materials to string the beads
Scissors

Photo by Tim Athey

BUTTERFLY WINGS

Purpose: feel still inside

Lie down comfortably and close your eyes.
Imagine that you are relaxing in a meadow on a warm day.

Notice the color of the summer sky overhead.
Feel the soft grass under your body.

Watch the fluffy clouds floating by.
Breathe in and smell the pine trees in the air.

Feel a cool summer breeze on your face.
Listen to the insects in the grass.

Smell the wild flowers and the clover.
Feel the warm sunshine all over your body.

Listen to the chirping of the birds in the trees.
Watch a giant butterfly nearby.

Notice the colors of its wings in the sunlight.
See how gently it moves.

It is about to land on your knee. Lie very still.
It will stay right there if you're quiet.

Now the butterfly wants to rest on your shoulder.
Be very still.   Breathe very gently.

Enjoy being peaceful together.   Shhh... let the butterfly go to sleep.

From *Taming Your Dragons* by M. Belknap. Page 33. Reprinted by permission of
Martha Belknap, 1170 Dixon Road/Gold Hill, Boulder, CO 80302.

CONCEPTS OF SELF-LOVE

What happened to you, not who you are, makes you angry, fearful, greedy, mean, anxious, etc. We learned behaviors in order to survive. We were taught to hate those behaviors and to see them as signs of our badness. Yet we must keep doing them because they still mean survival to us, and we hate ourselves for doing them.

THE TRAP:

    I believe I must be this way to survive.

    I hate myself for being this way.

THE RESULT:

    self-hate = survival

    survival = self-hate

It is a blessing to be confused. Confusion is the result of attempting to cling to illusion in the face of what you are seeing to be true for you. If you will continue to look, the confusion will give way to clarity. And the clarity is compassion.

SOME OF THE FORMS SELF-HATE TAKES

*SABOTAGE

    You try to do something good for yourself or for someone else and somehow manage to turn the whole thing against yourself. You keep doing the very things you didn't want to do or don't approve of, and you can't seem to figure out how you do that. It's a perfect system for self-hate because:

        1) You're operating out of an ideal.

        2) You don't live up to your ideal.

        3) You can't figure out what you're doing wrong.

*TAKING BLAME BUT NOT CREDIT

    If something goes well, it's a gift from God. If it goes badly, it's all your fault. And even if you do take a little credit for something, you can always avoid feeling good about it by finding what could have been done better.

*BLAMING OTHERS

    Self-hating and "other" hating are the same thing. Whether you are hateful toward others or hating yourself directly, it's self-hate—you are always the recipient.

*KEEPING SECRETS

> You don't let other people know what's going on inside you so that you can be in there beating yourself with it.

*HARBORING SECRET WOUNDS

> You review old hurts and injustices rather than being present to yourself now.

*NOT BEING ABLE TO RECEIVE

> Gifts, compliments, help, favors, praise, etc. are things you have difficulty allowing yourself to have.

*SEEING WHAT IS WRONG WITH EVERYTHING

> Your habit is to find fault, criticize, judge and compare. Remember, what <u>is</u>, is all that is. The alternate reality in which everything exists is only in your mind, and it exists primarily to torture you.

*ATTEMPTING TO BE PERFECT

*BEING ACCIDENT PRONE

> Your attention is so often focused on some other time, person or thing that you injure yourself in the present. You don't feel you deserve your attention. Others are more important.

*CONTINUING TO PUT YOURSELF IN ABUSIVE SITUATIONS

> Even if you realize that you have this pattern, your fear and self-hate are too strong to let you break out of it.

*MAINTAINING AN UNCOMFORTABLE PHYSICAL POSITION

> You hold your shoulders in a way that creates pain. You clench your teeth. You "sit small" on the bus so as not to intrude into anyone else's space. You continue to sit in an uncomfortable chair at work because you don't want to make waves.

*MAINTAINING AN UNCOMFORTABLE MENTAL POSITION

> Clinging to "shoulds": "It's not right to be happy when there is so much suffering in the world." "People should say please and thank you." "Children deserve to have two parents."

YOU CAN LISTEN TO VOICES THAT SAY THERE IS SOMETHING WRONG WITH YOU, IT'S ACTUALLY VERY HELPFUL TO BE AWARE OF THEM,

JUST DON'T BELIEVE THEM!

Most of what we have been TAUGHT TO BELIEVE.....

we had to be TAUGHT TO BELIEVE

BECAUSE * IT * ISN'T * TRUE

This is why children have to be conditioned so heavily!
WE WOULD NEVER HAVE REACHED THESE CONCLUSIONS ON OUR OWN!

If we could for a moment look at what we've been taught to believe with an unconditioned mind, we would see that not only is it not true, it's absurd.
So, what happened?

1) THE CHILD HAS A NEED

> Example: The child is afraid. Fear becomes a "subpersonality," a permanent aspect of this child's personality; a defense mechanism; a part of the child's survival system.

2) THE NEED IS REJECTED

> The need does not get met by the person who is looked to to meet it. The child is traumatized when this happens. The trauma/rejection becomes a subpersonality.

3) The child comes up with a BEHAVIOR as a means to survival in order to get the need met.

> Example: If the child is afraid of the dark, she/he will get up and sneak a flashlight into the bed. This behavior becomes a subpersonality.

4) The child identifies with the authority figure who didn't meet the need and, at the same time, identifies with the part who was rejected.

The belief that is born is:

"There must be something wrong with me. That's why they are treating me this way. It's my fault. It's not their fault; there can't be anything wrong with them because my survival depends on them."

THIS IS THE BIRTH OF SELF-HATE

5) The child decides to be PERFECT, to do everything right, to be really good in order to be loved. There is no choice about this; the child's survival depends on it.

> "They don't love me because there is something wrong with me. If I just do it right and never let that happen again, then they'll love me."

THIS SELF-TALK MAINTAINS SELF-HATE.

6) "THE JUDGE" as a subpersonality is born to make sure that the child is perfect and right and good in order to survive. The birth of the judge guarantees the continued existence of self-hate.

> This process is constantly repeating up through about age 7 when, it is said, we are completely socialized. After that, the judge is tenured and guaranteed a full-time job.

> During this process we have concluded that
> needs are bad,
> we are bad for having them.
> And, of course, we have them anyway.

APPRECIATING OURSELVES

We are the greatest thing that will ever happen to us. Believe it. It makes life much easier.

-Codependent No More

It is time to stop this nonsense of running around picking on ourselves.

We may have walked through much of our life apologizing for ourselves either directly or indirectly—feeling less than valuable than others, believing that they know better than we do, and believing that somehow others are meant to be here and we are not.

We have a right to be here.
We have a right to be ourselves.

We are here. There is a purpose, a reason, and an intention for our life. We do not have to apologize for being here or being who we are.

We are good enough, and deserving.

Others do not have our magic. We have our magic. It is in us.

It doesn't matter what we've done in our past. We all have a past, woven with mistakes, successes, and learning experiences. We have a right to our past. It is ours. It has worked to shape and form us. As we progress on this journey, we shall see how each of our experiences will be turned around and used for good.

We have already spent too much time being ashamed, being apologetic, and doubting the beauty of ourselves. Be done with it. Let it go. It is an unnecessary burden. Others have rights, but so do we. We are neither less than nor more than. We are equal. We are who we are. That is who we were created and intended to be.

That, my friend, is a wonderful gift.

God, help me own my power to love and appreciate myself. Help me give myself validity instead of looking to others to do that.

From *The Language of Letting Go: Daily Meditations for Codependents* by M. Beattie. Page 80.
Copyright 1990 by Hazelden Foundation, Center City, MN. Reprinted by permission.

WHAT IS SELF-LOVE?

Self-love is acknowledging and honoring yourself.

Self-love is surrounding yourself with people who nourish you.

Self-love is developing your creative drives.

Self-love is talking to yourself gently and lovingly.

Self-love is surrounding yourself with beauty.

Self-love is creating an abundance of friends.

Self-love is having confidence in your abilities.

Self-love is giving yourself pleasure without guilt.

Self-love is loving your body and seeing only its good qualities.

Self-love is letting yourself succeed.

Self-love is letting others in instead of submitting to loneliness.

Self-love is following your intuition.

Self-love is making your own rules responsibly.

Self-love is seeing your own perfection.

Self-love is taking credit for what you did.

Self-love is trusting yourself.

Self-love is nourishing yourself with good food and good ideas.

Self-love is getting a massage frequently.

Self-love is seeing yourself as equal to others.

Self-love is forgiving yourself.

Self-love is letting in affection.

Self-love is authority over yourself; not giving it away to another.

Self-love is becoming your own approving inner parent.

Self-love is turning all your negative thoughts into positive affirmations.

Self-love is speaking your truth.

Self-love is owning your own power.

TRUST

Purpose of Session:
1. Increase trust and cohesion among members
2. Explore concept of trusting self and others
3. Identify ways to increase self-trust

Time	Activity	Purpose
5 minutes	Centering Activity: Silence Ask members to slow down their chatterbox and become aware of their body.	Become focused and present centered.
15 minutes	Circle of Personal Power	Allow members to share immediate thoughts and feelings.
2 minutes	Read "Trusting Ourselves" by Melody Beattie.	Affirm our trust in ourselves. Bring topic of trust into awareness and prompt discussion.
15 minutes	Process: What does it mean to not trust fear? To not trust panic? What are some specific ways in which we show trust in ourselves? (i.e., our decisions, acknowledging and following our intuition, setting boundaries, allowing intimacy into our lives).	Bring about the awareness of each member's trust level and begin sharing how we can trust ourselves more.

25 minutes	Activity: Sherpa Walk Exercise in trusting self and others, and becoming aware of the responsibility involved in trusting. (Facilitation guide on following page)	Offer opportunity for members to make choices for themselves around trust, and experience a sense of trust in others.
30 minutes	Process: Round. Which was more difficult for you: to be blind or to be the leader and why? Is that a familiar role for you in your life? In what ways? How does trusting yourself affect your relationship with others? With yourself? What are you doing in your life that is allowing you to trust yourself? Others?	Transfer the learning and awareness that took place to other areas of one's life. Explore trust in self and others.
5 minutes	Closing. Round. What is one thing you are willing to do this week to move toward self-trust?	Ask members to identify a goal for moving forward. Sharing these goals enables other members to draw from and reflect upon them.

MATERIALS NEEDED:

Blindfolds are optional (1 for every 2 people)
Journals/Pens
Man-made or natural obstacle course

INSTRUCTIONS FOR THE SHERPA WALK:

The Sherpa Walk is so-named in reference to natives of the Himalayas who serve as guides to climbers who are ascending peaks such as Mount Everest, many for the first time. The Sherpa Walk is an opportunity to explore one's own trust level and to experience trust in another. Ask members to get a partner. During this activity, one person in the pair will be blindfolded as the other leads her/him through obstacles. This is a silent activity so members will need to find another way to communicate than through voice. Facilitators will lead the group and serve as spotters through the obstacles. After a certain amount of time, stop the activity and ask partners to switch roles.

Safety considerations:
Through the philosophy of challenge by choice, members reserve the right to stop the activity at any time and remove their blindfold. It is recommended to simply ask members to close their eyes. This way they are in control and may feel safer. Anything that happens in the activity is an opportunity to learn from and process, especially in regard to trust. Consideration should be taken in choosing an environment and obstacles that will fit the physical and emotional challenges of the group. Members should be spotted through obstacles by facilitators and care taken to maintain the safety of members at all times.

Set Up:
Divide members into 2 groups, careful to ask if there are half who would be willing to be "blind" first. Prepare the blindfolded members separately by asking them to "listen" to what their partner is trying to communicate to them. Ask them to be open to the challenge and experience, and to the fear they may experience. Ask them to think about what they can do to remain safe in the activity. Remind them that the activity revolves around trust.

Prepare the leaders by reminding them they are responsible for the safety of their partners. They will need to find a way to communicate with their partners and to be observant of their reactions. Allow the sighted members to choose their partners by quietly taking their arm and following in line, 10 feet between each pair. Guide the pairs single file through obstacles such as under tables or over curbs, whatever you feel is appropriate to the setting. Natural obstacles outside provide a wider range of smells and sounds for the person who is blind. As each pair nears the end of the obstacles (usually based on time), form them in a circle. Ask the members who are blindfolded for a feeling word that describes how they felt during the activity. You may also ask if they knew who their partner was. Have their partner take off their blindfold and switch roles. New partners can be chosen if desired. Process the experience when both groups have completed the activity.

Adapted from *Silver Bullets* by K. Rohnke. Page 89.
Copyright 1984 by Kendall/Hunt Publishing Company.

TRUSTING OURSELVES

Trust can be one of the most confusing concepts in recovery. Who do we trust? For what?

The most important trust issue we face is learning to trust ourselves. The most detrimental thing that's happened to us is that we came to believe we couldn't trust ourselves.

There will be some who tell us we cannot trust ourselves, we are off base and out of whack. There are those who would benefit by our mistrusting ourselves.

Fear and doubt are our enemies. Panic is our enemy. Confusion is our opposition.

Self-trust is a healing gift we can give ourselves. How do we acquire it? We learn it. What do we do about our mistakes, about those times we thought we could trust ourselves but were wrong? We accept them, and trust ourselves anyway.

We know what is best for us. We know what is right for us. If we are wrong, if we need to change our mind, we will be guided into that... but only by trusting where we are today.

We can look to others for support and reinforcement, but trust in ourselves is essential.

Do not trust fear. Do not trust panic. We can trust ourselves, stand in our own truth, stand in our own light. We have it now. Already. We have all the light we need for today. And tomorrow's light shall be given to us then.

Trust ourselves, and we will know whom to trust. Trust ourselves, and we will know what to do.

When we feel we absolutely cannot trust ourselves, trust that God will guide us into truth. God, help me let go of fear, doubt, and confusion—the enemies of self-trust. Help me go forward in peace and confidence. Help me grow in trust for myself and You, one day at a time, one experience at a time.

CLOSING SESSION #1

Purpose of Session:
1. Provide closure of group and address feelings regarding closure
2. Revisit special memories and experiences from the group
3. Provide an opportunity for members to share "gifts" they have received from other members
4. Reinforce members' personal strengths

Time	Activity	Purpose
10 minutes	Centering Activity: Sentence completion in their journals—"I remember when...." Complete as many sentences as they can, recalling experiences that stood out for them throughout the group.	Focus group members. Begin closure process by asking members to recall important events that stood out for them.
20 minutes	Process sentence completions, asking members to stay in touch with their feelings and express them consciously. Personal sharing of memories. Ask members to share feelings regarding the ending of group.	Allow members to express emotions and possible fears about leaving close friends and the support of the group.
40 minutes	Activity: The Web (Facilitation guide on following page)	Draw closure to the group by relating the impact of each member to the closeness of the group. Bring the group deeper by asking them to share what was important for them in the group, emotions they experienced, and goals they have accomplished.

| 10 minutes | Good-byes between members. Variations include a group hug or other centering, affirming activities. | Time for members to say good-bye to individual members. |

MATERIALS NEEDED:

Yarn (multi-colored)
Scissors
Matches
Tin Can
Journals
Pens

INSTRUCTIONS FOR THE WEB:

Tie several different colors of yarn together (or obtain yarn already woven together with different colors). Ask members to sit in a circle, on the floor or in chairs, and process what feelings arise for members through each of these colors. Share the significance of the colors in that they represent all the various emotions we have experienced together in this group. Begin to form the web by tossing the ball of yarn to someone across the circle. Ask members as they receive the ball of yarn, to express the connection they have formed between the group and what they have achieved personally as a member of the group. Members continue to hold on to the yarn as it is passed to the person across from them, forming a star and resembling a web. Explore the similar characteristics of the group and the web.

One at a time allow members to cut from the web a piece of the group, as small or large as they need to take with them as a symbol of our connection and all it represents: emotions, goals, lessons, support, etc. Ask each member what it is they are keeping from the group. When each member is finished, take the remainder of the web and place it in a tin can (or other safe container suitable for burning in). Whether outside or with adequate ventilation, burn the remainder of the web, signifying to members that we may not need the group physically when what we need from each other is in our hearts.

Photo by Tim Athey

CLOSING SESSION #2

Purpose of Session:
1. Provide closure to group and address feelings regarding closure
2. Create a symbolic quilt of what members have experienced in group to preserve those feelings in a visual and kinesthetic way
3. Allow members to express to others their feelings and wishes for them

Time	Activity	Purpose
5 minutes	Centering Activity: Ask a group member to lead.	Focus group members.
45 minutes	EXPLANATION OF THE QUILT: Paint, draw, etc., in a square, a picture or symbol that represents your growth. Ask members to take turns working on the quilt and writing in journals. Ask them to be done with both in one hour when the group will process. WRITTEN EXERCISE IN JOURNALS: How is your life different after being in this group? What concrete tools have you gained? What will you miss most about group? What, if anything, would you like to tell the group or a specific member?	Begin closure process by allowing members time to reflect on how their experience in group has affected them, and what specifically is different. Also gives members time to reflect on the role other members have played in their growth. Doing both activities simultaneously allows for fluent processing at the end of the session and completion of the quilt.

| 35 minutes | Process: Ask members to share what they have experienced for themselves and with others in the group and to share what concrete tools they are taking with them. Allow members to share feelings with the group and the significance of their square. Give attention to feelings about leaving the group. | Allow expression of feelings and thoughts about the closure of group, celebrating each other's growth and sharing their symbol of growth as signified in the quilt. |
| 5 minutes | Closing. Allow members to have time to say individual good-byes. | Allow for closure with individuals. |

MATERIALS NEEDED: (for a 9-square quilt)

Batting	white cloth	10 in. x 12 in.	(9 of them)
Scissors	colored border	36 in. x 5 in.	(4 of them)
Needle		42 in. x 5 in.	(4 of them)
Quilting Thread	extreme border	36 in. x 4 in.	(2 of them)
Rod to hang quilt		42 in. x 4 in.	(2 of them)
	cloth for backing	40 in. x 46 in.	

DIRECTIONS FOR QUILT:

Sew colored border onto white squares. Allow members to paint on separate squares. Allow to dry flat for 2 days. Choose backing and place batting between quilt and backing. Pin down. Start in the middle of the quilt. Quilt, or simply sew by hand small stitches around the white borders. Apply trim (extreme border) and a sleeve to hang from. Also possible to adjust these quilt squares so participants can take them home with them.

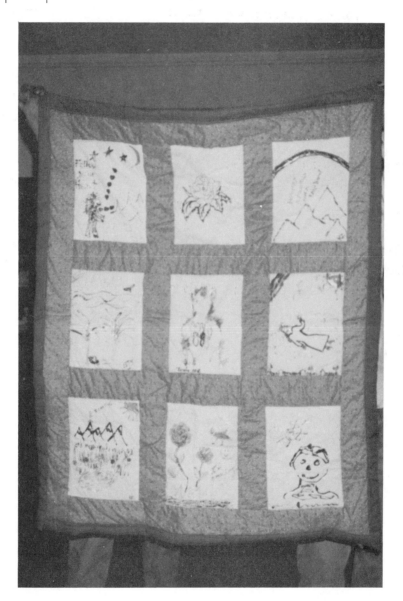

Photo by Karen M. Finch

SECTION FIVE

CLOSURE

Photo by Tim Athey

CLOSURE

In keeping with The K.E.Y. Group session plans, I began this book with a dedication, to center you and to get your attention. I walked you through background theories and their relevance to the activities presented in each session. I included information and examples, to aid you in the processing of these experiences. Now it is time for me to provide some closure, for you and also for me, as The K.E.Y. Group has been a big part of my life for the past two years.

When I look back over my experience leading The K.E.Y. Group, I realize the profound impact of owning one's "Power." Some do not like the concept of power and want no part of it. It is true that in our world, "power" has some negative connotations and often implies control over others. The power I speak of in The K.E.Y. Group is something entirely different. This kind of power has nothing to do with anyone else. It is not the ability to get others to do what you want them to do, but rather the ability to get yourself to do what you want to do. It's the kind of power that leaves you free, because you no longer expect the world to take care of you. If you do not own this kind of power, I believe you can lose your sense of peace, always waiting for someone to come by and hold your rope, as in "The Bridge" (Friedman, 1990).

One member shared her experience in the group through a metaphor with her children. She stated:

> I have two young children, a 7-year-old boy and a 10-year-old girl. The 7-year-old was constantly running to me when his sister was picking on him. My normal response was to address the 10-year-old and somehow get her to stop.
>
> One day I realized, more for myself, what was happening. I could punish her all I wanted and the teasing would not stop. I began to teach my boy about his choices: to not play with her, to leave when he was not enjoying it, or even to fight back. I tried to involve him in the consequences of his choices.

> The K.E.Y. Group made me aware of my responsibility in relationships, in family, at work.... There is both a great sadness for me, and a tremendous joy, that my children will learn this painful lesson thirty years earlier than I.
>
> -Kelly, K.E.Y. Group member

This is the place many K.E.Y. Group members have come from. A place of vulnerability and self-doubt. In 1995, The K.E.Y. Group was nominated for The Marshall's Domestic Peace Prize for its innovative efforts to help prevent and reduce domestic violence. The group has clearly made an impact upon how members view their choices in life, and what it means for them if they choose to accept the responsiblity for others. Overcoming the guilt of no longer being people-pleasing was a common issue for many members. Their worth had been tied up in being needed. One member shared with the group her most meaningful insight:

> My partner and I have been constant companions for a long time. Being alone was a scary thought. I believed for a long time that I needed him. What I realize now is, I don't **need** him. I love him, and I would be very sad without him, but I don't need him to live my life. Sort of a freeing thing to take that responsiblity back and live with the knowing that I could handle it.
>
> Karina, K.E.Y. Group member

The following are excerpts from letters K.E.Y. Group members submitted in support of the group's impact on their lives:

> The K.E.Y. Group has helped me to find a balance that I can maintain and be happy with. The fear I held for my children and myself after leaving a very physically and emotionally abusive husband paralyzed me. I give immense credit to Karen and The K.E.Y. Group for enabling me to be a trusting, happy, productive, and strong woman and mother.

The Group continues to be a very important part of my life, not only to help me thrive instead of survive, but also to keep the focus on myself and continue to grow. Due to The K.E.Y. Group, violence is no longer a part of my life or my children's.

-Kim, K.E.Y. Group member

The K.E.Y. Group has advanced me in discovering my worth as a woman. I radiate self-love and a positive self-image now. I have shared The K.E.Y. Group handouts with my male friend and ex-perpetrator, who also has grown and integrated this healthy way of thinking into his life. Therefore, I believe The K.E.Y. Group can be an essential part of life not only to wo men, but also to men.

The K.E.Y. Group has certainly helped me to stop people-pleasing. My thoughts, my dress, and my worth as a woman cannot be changed any more by other peoples' opinions, only my own. I stand on my own two feet these days and more importantly, I really like myself. I am able to recognize abuse immediately and I now have the "tools" to remove myself from the situation. I know about and trust my feelings. If things don't feel right, I can refrain. The K.E.Y. Group has been an important part in all of my realizations and will continue to remain the "KEY" in living my new, healthy lifestyle.

Sabrina, K.E.Y. Group member

Prior to attending The K.E.Y. Group, I was entering the 8th year of an extremely emotionally abusive relationship. I blamed him and everything around me for my misery. I deserved the abuse because I was undeserving of more. He was my life and my identity. I desperately needed his love, acceptance, and approval to ease my guilt and shame.

Because of The K.E.Y. Group, my life is different. I have been out of that abusive relationship for over two years now and have entered a new and healthy one. The group taught me to focus on myself because I can only change myself, and that by changing me, I change my relationship, or gain the courage to leave it. It taught me that I have an intuition that will never fail me and that I need to listen to it. I've learned how to reprogram my negative chatterbox in my mind through positive affirmations to raise my self-esteem and self-love. I've learned that I deserve an abuse-free life.

The K.E.Y. Group has eliminated domestic violence from my life because I am able to respond differently to situations. It was hard to change my thoughts about myself. I am still working on it daily, just by being conscious. The K.E.Y. Group was difficult, challenging, and I LOVED it!!!

Lynn, K.E.Y. Group member

WHEN I DARE TO BE POWERFUL -
TO USE MY STRENGTH IN THE SERVICE
OF MY VISION, THEN IT BECOMES LESS
IMPORTANT WHETHER I AM AFRAID.

Audre Lorde

REFERENCES

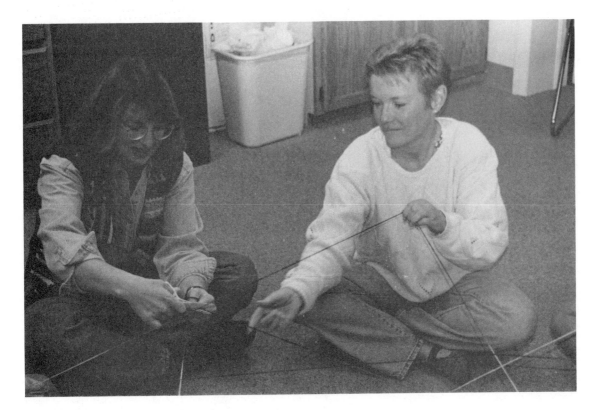

Photo by Tim Athey

Angus, L. E., & Rennie, D. L. (1989). Envisioning the representational world: The client's experience of metaphoric expression in psychotherapy. *Psychotherapy, 26,* 372-382.

Aroaz, D. (1985). *The new hypnosis.* New York: Brunner/Mazel.

Atwood, L. E., & Levine, L. B. (1990). The therapeutic metaphor. *The Australian Journal of Clinical Hypnotherapy and Hypnosis, 11*(2), 17-40.

Bacon, S. (1983). *The conscious use of metaphor in Outward Bound.* Denver, CO: Colorado Outward Bound School.

Bacon, S. (1987). *The evolution of the Outward Bound process.* Greenwich, CT: Outward Bound.

Bandler, R. (1985). *Using your brain for a change.* Moab, UT: Real People Press.

Bandler, R., & Grinder, J. (1975). *Patterns of hypnotic techniques of Milton Erickson, M. D.* (Vol. 1). Cupertino, CA: Meta Publications.

Beattie, M. (1990). *The language of letting go: Daily meditations for codependents.* Center City, MN: Hazelden Foundation.

Beck, A. T. (1973). *The diagnosis and management of depression.* Philadelphia, PA: University of Pennsylvania Press.

Belknap, M. (1989). *Taming your dragons.* Available from the author: 1170 Dixon Road, Gold Hill, Boulder, CO 80302.

Berg, I. K. (1994). *Family based services: A solution-focused approach.* New York: W. W. Norton.

Bowman, G. (1992). Using therapeutic metaphor in adjustment counseling. *Journal of Visual Impairment and Blindness, 86*(10), 440-442.

A Center for the Practice of Zen Buddhist Meditation. Keep It Simple Books.
P.O. Box 91
Mountain View, CA 94042
(800) 200-6334:

> The key and the name of the key is willingness.
> That which you are seeking is causing you to seek.
> The how you do anything is how you do everything workbook.
> The depression book. Depression as an opportunity for spiritual growth.
> There is nothing wrong with you.

Chapman, S., McPhee, P., & Proudman, B. (1992). What is experiential education? *Journal of Experiential Education, 15*(2), 16-23.

Combs, G., & Freedman, J. (1990). *Symbol, story and ceremony: Using metaphor in individual and family therapy.* New York: W. W. Norton.

Davis, M., & Eshelman, E. (1988). *The relaxation and stress reduction workbook.* Oakland, CA: New Harbinger.

de Shazer, S. (1982). *Patterns of brief family therapy.* New York: Guilford.

de Shazer, S. (1985). *Keys to solution in brief therapy.* New York: Guilford.

de Shazer, S. (1988). *Clues: Investigating solutions in brief therapy.* New York: W. W. Norton.

Duerk, J. (1989). *Circle of stones: Woman's journey to herself.* San Diego, CA: LuraMedia.

Fisher, B. (1978). *When your relationship ends.* Boulder, CO: Family Relations Learning Center, Inc.

Friedman, E. H. (1990). *Friedman's fables.* New York: Guilford.

Gass, M. A. (1991). Enhancing metaphor development in adventure therapy programs. *Journal of Experiential Education, 14*(20), 6-13.

Gass, M. A. (1993). *Adventure therapy: Therapeutic applications of adventure programming .* Dubuque, IA: Kendall/Hunt.

Gass, M. A., & Gillis, H. L. (1995). Focusing on the "solution" rather than the "problem": Empowering client change in adventure experiences. *Journal of Experiential Education, 18*(2), 63-69.

Gass, M. A., & Priest, S. (1993). Using metaphors and isomorphs to transfer learning in adventure education. *Journal of Adventure Education, 10*(4), 18-24.

Gerstein, J. S. (1996). *Experiential family counseling. A practitioner's guide to orientation materials, warm-ups, family building initiatives and review exercises* (2nd ed.). Dubuque, IA: Kendall/Hunt.

Gillis, H. L., & Bonney, W. C. (1986). Group counseling with couples or families: Adding adventure activities. *Journal for Specialists in Group Work, 11*(4), 213-220.

Gordon, D. (1978). *Therapeutic metaphors.* Cupertino, CA: Meta Publications.

Haley, J. (1973). *Uncommon therapy: The psychiatric techniques of Milton Erickson.* New York: W. W. Norton.

Hendrix, D. H. (1992). Metaphors as nudges toward understanding in mental health counseling. *Journal of Mental Health Counseling, 14*(2), 234-242.

Jeffers, S. (1987). *Feel the fear and do it anyway.* Orlando, FL: Harcourt Brace.

Jooste, E. T., & Cleaver, G. (1992). Metaphors and metaphoric objects. *Journal of Phenomenological Psychology, 23*(2), 136-148.

Knapp, C. C. (1989). *The art and science of processing experience* (pp. 1-16). Hamilton, MA: Project Adventure.

Knapp, C. C. (1992). *Lasting lessons: A teacher's guide to processing an experience.* Charleston, SC: Appalachia Educational Laboratory.

Kolb, D. (1976). *Experiential learning: Experience as the source of learning.* Englewood Cliffs, NJ: Prentice Hall.

Luria, A. (1973). *The working brain.* New York: Basic Books.

Nadler, R., & Luckner, J. (1992). *Processing the experience: Theory and practice.* Dubuque, IA: Kendall/Hunt.

Priest, S. (1989). A model of G.I.F.T. *The Outdoor Communicator, 20*(1), 8-13.

Priest, S., & Gass, M. A. (1994). Frontloading with paradox and double binds in adventure education facilitation. *Journal of Adventure Education, 11*(1), 18-24.

Quinsland, L. K., & Van Ginkel, A. (1984). How to process experience. *The Journal of Experiential Education, 7*(2), 8-13.

Rohnke, K. (1984). *Silver bullets.* Dubuque, IA: Kendall/Hunt.

Rohnke, K. (1991). *The bottomless bag.* Dubuque, IA: Kendall/Hunt.

Rossi, E. L. (Ed.). (1980). *The collected papers of Milton H. Erickson on hypnosis.* New York: Irvington.

Schoel, J., Prouty, D., & Radcliffe, P. (1988). *Islands of healing: A guide to adventure based counseling.* Hamilton, MA: Project Adventure.

Strong, T. (1989). Metaphors and client change in counseling. *International Journal for the Advancement of Counseling, 12*(3), 203-213.

Tuckerman, B. W. (1965). Development sequence in small groups. *Psychological Bulletin, 63*(6).

Williams, M. (1991). *The velveteen rabbit.* Morris Plains, NJ: Unicorn Publishing.

Zeig, J. K., & Gilligan, S. G. (1990). *Brief therapy. Myths, methods and metaphors.* New York: Brunner/Mazel.

ABOUT THE AUTHOR

Karen M. Finch received her M.Ed. in Counseling from Colorado State University. She has worked with women, victims of crime, families, couples, and people with disabilities since 1985, using experiential learning in group facilitation. Most recently she worked as a counselor at Crossroads Safehouse for Battered Women in Fort Collins, Colorado .

Karen and her husband Brad spend their free time adventuring in the outdoors and enjoying their dogs and llamas at their new home in Mancos, Colorado.

Association for Experiential Education
Publications

2305 Canyon Blvd., Ste. #100, Boulder, CO 80302-5651, USA

Tel. 303-440-8844   FAX 303-440-9581

e-mail: info@aee.org

* Books marked with an asterisk (*) can be ordered directly from Kendall/Hunt Publishing by calling (800) 228-0810 or 319-589-1000. To receive your AEE member discount, when calling, please reference AEE and have your membership number ready .

BOOKS

ADVENTURE EDUCATION
Available from Venture Publishing by calling 814-234-4561 -- AEE members receive a discount

John C. Miles and Simon Priest

ISBN #0-910251-39-8

This book provides the first comprehensive examination of all aspects of adventure education from history, to philosophy, to leadership, to administration. In 53 chapters, it brings together the ideas of many practitioners of adventure education programming to reveal the extent of the literature in the field providing insight into every aspect of this growing movement.

Member $25.55 / Non Member $31.95

ADVENTURE THERAPY: Therapeutic Applications of Adventure Programming *

Michael A. Gass, Ph.D.

ISBN #0-8403-8272-3

This valuable resource book contains writings by Dr. Gass and other respected practitioners in the growing field of therapeutic adventure programming.

BOOK OF METAPHORS, VOLUME II *

Michael A. Gass, Ph.D.

ISBN #0-7872-0306-8

The use of metaphors in adventure programming often serves as a key for producing lasting functional change for clients. Topics covered include steps for framing experiences, verbal introductions, debriefing, and methods for facilitating adventure experiences.

ETHICAL ISSUES IN EXPERIENTIAL EDUCATION, SECOND EDITION *

Jasper S. Hunt, Jr.

ISBN #0-8403-9038-6

An examination of the current ethical issues in the field of adventure programming and experiential education. Examples of topics include ethical theory, informed consent, sexual issues, student rights, environmental concerns, and programming practices.

EXPERIENCE AND THE CURRICULUM*

Bert Horwood, editor

ISBN #0-7872-1596-1

An anthology where teachers' voices, raised out of hard-won experience and filtered through thoughtful, critical perspectives, provide insiders' views of practice. Unlike the restricted notion that the "experience" in experiential education must comprise some kind of physical adventure, in these stories active experience includes reading and writing, families, the community and classroom work, as well as out-of-school events.

EXPERIENTIAL EDUCATION IN HIGH SCHOOL: Life in the Walkabout Program

Bert Horwood, with a foreword by Maurice Gibbons

ISBN #0-9293-6104-0

This book is a stirring ethnography of Jefferson County Open High School, an institution based on the revolutionary idea of high school as a right of passage from adolescence to adulthood.

EXPERIENTIAL LEARNING IN SCHOOLS AND HIGHER EDUCATION *

Richard J. Kraft and James Kielsmeier, editors

ISBN #0-7872-0183-9

This updated and expanded anthology addresses the role of experiential education at all levels of schooling. This book is a must for educators, school board members, administrators, professors, and researchers who are still striving to improve education for all our children, young people, and adults.

THE K.E.Y. (KEEP EXPLORING YOURSELF) GROUP: An Experiential Personal-Growth Group Manual*

Karen M. Finch

The K.E.Y. Group is a manual intended for the purpose of facilitating an experiential personal growth group. Essentially, The K.E.Y. Group focuses on taking care of oneself and introduces, in an enjoyable way, the various tools needed to do that. It consists of information and affirmations integrated into an experiential format for addressing specific issues. The K.E.Y. Group is comprised of 20 sessions that are complete with centering activities, experiential activities, processing questions, and information sheets on topics such as Empowerment, Setting Boundaries, Fear, Trust, Depression as an Opportunity for Growth, and more.

THE THEORY OF EXPERIENTIAL EDUCATION, THIRD EDITION *

Karen Warren, Mitchell Sakofs and Jasper S. Hunt, Jr., editors

ISBN #0-7872-0262-2

The third edition of this groundbreaking book looks at the theoretical foundations of experiential education from a philosophical, historical, psychological, social, and ethical perspective. The aim of the book is to encourage readers to think about *why* they are doing *what* they are doing.

WOMEN'S VOICES IN EXPERIENTIAL EDUCATION*

Karen Warren, editor

ISBN #0-7872-2059-0

A celebration of women's voices in experiential education and a contribution to the dialogue about gender issues in the profession. The book includes feminist analysis of many topics in experiential education, particularly as it applies to the outdoors and adventure education, as well as practical examples of how women's experiences can contribute to the field as a whole.

OTHER PUBLICATIONS

ADVENTURE PROGRAM RISK MANAGEMENT REPORT 1995: Incident Data and Narratives from 1989 & 1990

Jeff Liddle and Steve Storck, editors

An excellent resource for anyone, from administrators to instructors, charged with managing risk in adventure programming. An annual periodical reviewing the prior year's incident data in adventure programming. A joint project of AEE and the Wilderness Risk Managers Committee.

CONFERENCE PROCEEDINGS MANUALS: 1995-1996

A collection of abstracts from the various workshops presented at International AEE Conferences.

GUIDE TO EXPERIENTIAL EDUCATION RESOURCES

A "catalog" with a comprehensive listing of books, journals, organizations, newsletters, and other resources related to the many areas of experiential education. Items are classified and cross-referenced by subject, including Adventure Education; Games, Activities & Initiatives; Youth; Professional Organizations; Technical/Risk Management; Therapeutic Applications; International/Multicultural, and more.

MANUAL OF ACCREDITATION STANDARDS FOR ADVENTURE PROGRAMS 1995

ISBN #0-9293-61-13-X

The most recent issue of the guidelines used to review and accredit programs through AEE's *Program Accreditation Services*. The *Manual of Accreditation Standards* represents the collective experience of program professionals who have designed and run the activities presented in this book.

PERIODICALS

JOBS CLEARINGHOUSE
One of the most comprehensive and widely used monthly listings of full-time, part-time, and seasonal job and internship opportunities in the experiential/adventure education field. One-year subscriptions and single issues available.

THE JOURNAL OF EXPERIENTIAL EDUCATION (JEE)
A professional journal for people in the field of experiential education and adventure education. Three issues per year. (Also available: back issues and multi-volume sets.) Included with AEE membership.

JEE MULTI-VOLUME SETS
An invaluable reference tool for anyone in the field of experiential education, and a must for your library, school, or organization's collection.
All-Volume Collection
One-Volume Sets (3 issues) for any year from 1978-1995

AEE JOURNAL INDEX
Includes all volumes from 1978-1995, classified by subject, title, and author.

DIRECTORIES

DIRECTORY OF EXPERIENTIAL THERAPY AND ADVENTURE-BASED COUNSELING PROGRAMS
edited by Jackie Gerstein, Ed.D.
A complete biographical breakdown of each organization listed, this directory identifies those programs which use adventure and experiential activities with special needs populations for therapeutic purposes. Lists 257 organizations whose missions include utilizing experiential/adventure exercises as therapeutic and educational tools. (1992)

EXPERIENCE-BASED TRAINING AND DEVELOPMENT: Directory of Programs
edited by David Agran, Dan Garvey, Todd Miner, and Simon Priest
A descriptive listing of over 90 training and development programs in North America and abroad. Also includes chapters on shopping for a program provider, descriptions of activity categories, and services and resources. (1993)

SCHOOLS & COLLEGES DIRECTORY
Provides information about many schools, colleges, and universities that have programs or offer degrees related to the field of outdoor experiential education. Listings include programs in high schools and independent organizations as well as institutions of higher learning. Most entries list programs offered, contact names and addresses, and degrees available.

The Association for Experiential Education (AEE)

The Association for Experiential Education (AEE) is a not-for-profit, international, professional organization committed to furthering experiential-based teaching and learning in a culture that is increasingly "information-rich but experience-poor." AEE sponsors local, regional, and international conferences and publishes the *Journal of Experiential Education*, the *Jobs Clearinghouse*, directories of programs and services, and a wide variety of books and periodicals to support educators, trainers, practitioners, students, and advocates.

To receive additional information about the Association for Experiential Education, call or write: AEE, 2305 Canyon Blvd., Ste. #100, Boulder, Colorado, USA 80302-5651, (303) 440-8844, (303) 440-9541 (FAX), e-mail: info@aee.org

Please send information on the following:
- ❏ Membership in AEE
- ❏ Program Accreditation Services
- ❏ Conferences
- ❏ Publications List

Please send the following AEE-K/H books:

Qty.	ISBN #	Author & Title	Price AEE Member	Non-Member	Total
	0-7872-2222-4	Finch/*The K.E.Y. Group*	16.00	21.95	
	0-8403-8272-3	Gass/*Adventure Therapy*	23.00	29.95	
	0-7872-0306-8	Gass/*Book of Metaphors, Volume II*	23.00	28.95	
	0-8403-9038-6	Hunt/*Ethical Issues in Experiential Education, Second Edition*	16.00	23.00	
	0-7872-1596-1	Horwood/*Experience and the Curriculum*	24.00	29.95	
	0-7872-0183-9	Kraft & Kielsmeier/*Experiential Learning in Schools and Higher Education*	30.00	38.00	
	0-7872-0262-2	Warren et al./*The Theory of Experiential Education, Third Edition*	24.00	35.95	
	0-7872-2059-0	Warren/*Women's Voices in Experiential Education*	19.00	23.95	
AL, AZ, CA, CO, FL, GA, IA, IL, KY, LA, MA, MD, MI, NJ, NY, PA, TN, TX, & WI orders, please add your appropriate sales tax.				Tax:	
Please add $4.00 shipping and handling for the first book. Add $.50 for each additional book ordered. International customers—call for estimate.				Shipping:	
				Total:	

Ship To:

Name _____

Address_____

City_____ State_____ Zip_____

Phone (_____) _____

AEE Membership number_____

Payment:
- ❏ Check enclosed
- ❏ Purchase Order

Charge to: ❏ American Express ❏ Visa ❏ MasterCard

Card #_____ Exp._____

Name as it appears on card: _____

Signature_____

(Signature required for all charge orders.)

Copy or detach this form and either:

Mail: Kendall/Hunt Publishing Company
Customer Service
4050 Westmark Drive
P.O. Box 1840
Dubuque, IA 52004-1840, USA

Toll-Free FAX: 1-800-772-9165
(24 hours a day/7 days a week)
International FAX: 1-319-589-1046

For a complete listing of available AEE publications and membership information, please see pages 177-180 in this book or contact AEE at the phone number or address listed above.